THE HISTORY & CULTURE
of NATIVE AMERICANS

The Nez Perce

THE HISTORY & CULTURE of NATIVE AMERICANS

THE HISTORY & CULTURE of NATIVE AMERICANS

The Nez Perce

NANCY BONVILLAIN

Series Editor
PAUL C. ROSIER

CHELSEA HOUSE
PUBLISHERS
An imprint of Infobase Publishing

The Nez Perce
Copyright © 2011 by Infobase Publishing

Chelsea House
An imprint of Infobase Publishing
132 West 31st Street
New York NY 10001

Library of Congress Cataloging-in-Publication Data

Bonvillain, Nancy.
  The Nez Perce / Nancy Bonvillain.
    p. cm. — (The history and culture of Native Americans)
  Includes bibliographical references and index.
  ISBN 978-1-60413-791-0 (hardcover)
  1. Nez Percé Indians—History—Juvenile literature. 2. Nez Percé Indians—Social life and customs—Juvenile literature. I. Title. II. Series.

  E99.N5B66 2011
  979.5004'9741—dc22   2010016114

Chelsea House books are available at special discounts when purchased in bulk quantities for businesses, associations, institutions, or sales promotions. Please call our Special Sales Department in New York at (212) 967-8800 or (800) 322-8755.

You can find Chelsea House on the World Wide Web at
http://www.chelseahouse.com

Text design by Lina Farinella
Cover design by Alicia Post
Composition by Newgen
Cover printed by Bang Printing, Brainerd, Minn.
Book printed and bound by Bang Printing, Brainerd, Minn.
Date printed: October 2010
Printed in the United States of America

10 9 8 7 6 5 4 3 2 1
This book is printed on acid-free paper.

Contents

Foreword
by Paul C. Rosier

Native American words, phrases, and tribal names are embedded in the very geography of the United States—in the names of creeks, rivers, lakes, cities, and states, including Alabama, Connecticut, Iowa, Kansas, Illinois, Missouri, Oklahoma, and many others. Yet Native Americans remain the most misunderstood ethnic group in the United States. This is a result of limited coverage of Native American history in middle schools, high schools, and colleges; poor coverage of contemporary Native American issues in the news media; and stereotypes created by Hollywood movies, sporting events, and TV shows.

Two newspaper articles about American Indians caught my eye in recent months. Paired together, they provide us with a good introduction to the experiences of American Indians today: first, how they are stereotyped and turned into commodities; and second, how they see themselves being a part of the United States and of the wider world. (Note: I use the terms *Native Americans* and *American Indians* interchangeably; both terms are considered appropriate.)

In the first article, "Humorous Souvenirs to Some, Offensive Stereotypes to Others," written by Carol Berry in *Indian Country Today,* I read that tourist shops in Colorado were selling "souvenir" T-shirts portraying American Indians as drunks. "My Indian name is Runs with Beer," read one T-shirt offered in Denver. According to the article, the T-shirts are "the kind of stereotype-reinforcing products also seen in nearby Boulder, Estes Park, and likely other Colorado communities, whether as part of the tourism trade or as everyday merchandise." No other ethnic group in the United States is stereotyped in such a public fashion. In addition, Native people are used to sell a range of consumer goods, including the Jeep Cherokee, Red Man chewing tobacco, Land O'Lakes butter, and other items that either objectify or insult them, such as cigar store Indians. As importantly, non-Indians learn about American Indian history and culture through sports teams such as the Atlanta Braves, Cleveland Indians, Florida State Seminoles, or Washington Redskins, whose name many American Indians consider a racist insult; dictionaries define *redskin* as a "disparaging" or "offensive" term for American Indians. When fans in Atlanta do their "tomahawk chant" at Braves baseball games, they perform two inappropriate and related acts: One, they perpetuate a stereotype of American Indians as violent; and two, they tell a historical narrative that covers up the violent ways that Georgians treated the Cherokee during the Removal period of the 1830s.

The second article, written by Melissa Pinion-Whitt of the San Bernardino *Sun* addressed an important but unknown dimension of Native American societies that runs counter to the irresponsible and violent image created by products and sporting events. The article, "San Manuels Donate $1.7 M for Aid to Haiti," described a Native American community that had sent aid to Haiti after it was devastated in January 2010 by an earthquake that killed more than 200,000 people, injured hundreds of thousands more, and destroyed the Haitian capital. The San Manuel Band of Mission Indians in California donated $1.7 million to help relief efforts in Haiti; San Manuel children held fund-raisers to collect additional donations. For the San Manuel Indians it was nothing new; in 2007 they had donated $1 million to help Sudanese refugees in Darfur. San Manuel also contributed $700,000 to relief efforts following Hurricane Katrina and Hurricane Rita, and donated $1 million in 2007 for wildfire recovery in Southern California.

Such generosity is consistent with many American Indian nations' cultural practices, such as the "give-away," in which wealthy tribal members give to the needy, and the "potlatch," a winter gift-giving ceremony and feast tradition shared by tribes in the

Pacific Northwest. And it is consistent with historical accounts of American Indians' generosity. For example, in 1847 Cherokee and Choctaw, who had recently survived their forced march on a "Trail of Tears" from their homelands in the American South to present-day Oklahoma, sent aid to Irish families after reading of the potato famine, which created a similar forced migration of Irish. A Cherokee newspaper editorial, quoted in Christine Kinealy's *The Great Irish Famine: Impact, Ideology, and Rebellion,* explained that the Cherokee "will be richly repaid by the consciousness of having done a good act, by the moral effect it will produce abroad." During and after World War II, nine Pueblo communities in New Mexico offered to donate food to the hungry in Europe, after Pueblo army veterans told stories of suffering they had witnessed while serving in the United States armed forces overseas. Considering themselves a part of the wider world, Native people have reached beyond their borders, despite their own material poverty, to help create a peaceful world community.

American Indian nations have demonstrated such generosity within the United States, especially in recent years. After the terrorist attacks of September 11, 2001, the Lakota Sioux in South Dakota offered police officers and emergency medical personnel to New York City to help with relief efforts; Indian nations across the country sent millions of dollars to help the victims of the attacks. As an editorial in the *Native American Times* newspaper explained on September 12, 2001, "American Indians love this country like no other. . . . Today, we are all New Yorkers."

Indeed, Native Americans have sacrificed their lives in defending the United States from its enemies in order to maintain their right to be both American and Indian. As the volumes in this series tell us, Native Americans patriotically served as soldiers (including as "code talkers") during World War I and World War II, as well as during the Korean War, the Vietnam War, and, after 9/11, the wars in Afghanistan and Iraq. Native soldiers, men and women, do so today by the tens of thousands because they believe in America, an

America that celebrates different cultures and peoples. Sgt. Leonard Gouge, a Muscogee Creek, explained it best in an article in *Cherokee News Path* in discussing his post-9/11 army service. He said he was willing to serve his country abroad because "by supporting the American way of life, I am preserving the Indian way of life."

This new Chelsea House series has two main goals. The first is to document the rich diversity of American Indian societies and the ways their cultural practices and traditions have evolved over time. The second goal is to provide the reader with coverage of the complex relationships that have developed between non-Indians and Indians over the past several hundred years. This history helps to explain why American Indians consider themselves both American and Indian and why they see preserving this identity as a strength of the American way of life, as evidence to the rest of the world that America is a champion of cultural diversity and religious freedom. By exploring Native Americans' cultural diversity and their contributions to the making of the United States, these volumes confront the stereotypes that paint all American Indians as the same and portray them as violent; as "drunks," as those Colorado T-shirts do; or as rich casino owners, as many news accounts do.

*   *   *

Each of the 14 volumes in this series is written by a scholar who shares my conviction that young adult readers are both fascinated by Native American history and culture and have not been provided with sufficient material to properly understand the diverse nature of this complex history and culture. The authors themselves represent a varied group that includes university teachers and professional writers, men and women, and Native and non-Native. To tell these fascinating stories, this talented group of scholars has examined an incredible variety of sources, both the primary sources that historical actors have created and the secondary sources that historians and anthropologists have written to make sense of the past.

Although the 14 Indian nations (also called tribes and communities) selected for this series have different histories and cultures, they all share certain common experiences. In particular, they had to face an American empire that spread westward in the eighteenth and nineteenth centuries, causing great trauma and change for all Native people in the process. Because each volume documents American Indians' experiences dealing with powerful non-Indian institutions and ideas, I outline below the major periods and features of federal Indian policy-making in order to provide a frame of reference for complex processes of change with which American Indians had to contend. These periods—Assimilation, Indian New Deal, Termination, Red Power, and Self-determination—and specific acts of legislation that define them—in particular the General Allotment Act, the Indian Reorganization Act, and the Indian Self-determination and Education Assistance Act—will appear in all the volumes, especially in the latter chapters.

In 1851, the commissioner of the federal Bureau of Indian Affairs (BIA) outlined a three-part program for subduing American Indians militarily and assimilating them into the United States: concentration, domestication, and incorporation. In the first phase, the federal government waged war with the American Indian nations of the American West in order to "concentrate" them on reservations, away from expanding settlements of white Americans and immigrants. Some American Indian nations experienced terrible violence in resisting federal troops and state militia; others submitted peacefully and accepted life on a reservation. During this phase, roughly from the 1850s to the 1880s, the U.S. government signed hundreds of treaties with defeated American Indian nations. These treaties "reserved" to these American Indian nations specific territory as well as the use of natural resources. And they provided funding for the next phase of "domestication."

During the domestication phase, roughly the 1870s to the early 1900s, federal officials sought to remake American Indians in the mold of white Americans. Through the Civilization Program, which actually started with President Thomas Jefferson, federal officials sent religious missionaries, farm instructors, and teachers to the newly created reservations in an effort to "kill the Indian to save the man," to use a phrase of that time. The ultimate goal was to extinguish American Indian cultural traditions and turn American Indians into Christian yeoman farmers. The most important piece of legislation in this period was the General Allotment Act (or Dawes Act), which mandated that American Indian nations sell much of their territory to white farmers and use the proceeds to farm on what was left of their homelands. The program was a failure, for the most part, because white farmers got much of the best arable land in the process. Another important part of the domestication agenda was the federal boarding school program, which required all American Indian children to attend schools to further their rejection of Indian ways and the adoption of non-Indian ways. The goal of federal reformers, in sum, was to incorporate (or assimilate) American Indians into American society as individual citizens and not as groups with special traditions and religious practices.

During the 1930s some federal officials came to believe that American Indians deserved the right to practice their own religion and sustain their identity as Indians, arguing that such diversity made America stronger. During the Indian New Deal period of the 1930s, BIA commissioner John Collier devised the Indian Reorganization Act (IRA), which passed in 1934, to give American Indian nations more power, not less. Not all American Indians supported the IRA, but most did. They were eager to improve their reservations, which suffered from tremendous poverty that resulted in large measure from federal policies such as the General Allotment Act.

Some federal officials opposed the IRA, however, and pushed for the assimilation of American Indians in a movement called Termination. The two main goals of Termination advocates, during the 1950s and 1960s, were to end (terminate) the federal reservation system and American Indians' political sovereignty derived from treaties and to relocate American Indians from rural reservations to urban areas. These coercive federal assimilation policies in turn generated resistance from Native Americans, including young activists who helped to create the so-called Red Power era of the 1960s and 1970s, which coincided with the African-American civil rights movement. This resistance led to the federal government's rejection of Termination policies in 1970. And in 1975 the U.S. Congress passed the Indian Self-determination and Education Assistance Act, which made it the government's policy to support American Indians' right to determine the future of their communities. Congress then passed legislation to help American Indian nations to improve reservation life; these acts strengthened American Indians' religious freedom, political sovereignty, and economic opportunity.

All American Indians, especially those in the western United States, were affected in some way by the various federal policies described above. But it is important to highlight the fact that each American Indian community responded in different ways to these pressures for change, both the detribalization policies of assimilation and the retribalization policies of self-determination. There is no one group of "Indians." American Indians were and still are a very diverse group. Some embraced the assimilation programs of the federal government and rejected the old traditions; others refused to adopt non-Indian customs or did so selectively, on their own terms. Most American Indians, as I noted above, maintain a dual identity of American and Indian.

Today, there are more than 550 American Indian (and Alaska Natives) nations recognized by the federal government. They have a legal and political status similar to states, but they have special rights and privileges that are the result of congressional acts and the hundreds of treaties that still govern federal-Indian relations today. In July 2008, the total population of American Indians (and Alaska Natives) was 4.9 million, representing about 1.6 percent of the United States population. The state with the highest number of American Indians is California, followed by Oklahoma, home to the Cherokee (the largest American Indian nation in terms of population), and then Arizona, home to the Navajo (the second-largest American Indian nation). All told, roughly half of the American Indian population lives in urban areas; the other half lives on reservations and in other rural parts of the country. Like all their fellow American citizens, American Indians pay federal taxes, obey federal laws, and vote in federal, state, and local elections; they also participate in the democratic processes of their American Indian nations, electing judges, politicians, and other civic officials.

This series on the history and culture of Native Americans celebrates their diversity and differences as well as the ways they have strengthened the broader community of America. Ronnie Lupe, the chairman of the White Mountain Apache government in Arizona, once addressed questions from non-Indians as to "why Indians serve the United States with such distinction and honor?" Lupe, a Korean War veteran, answered those questions during the Gulf War of 1991–1992, in which Native American soldiers served to protect the independence of the Kuwaiti people. He explained in "Chairman's Corner" in *The Fort Apache Scout* that "our loyalty to the United States goes beyond our need to defend our home and reservation lands. . . . Only a few in this country really understand that the indigenous people are a national treasure. Our values have the potential of creating the social, environmental, and spiritual healing that could make this country truly great."

—Paul C. Rosier
Associate Professor of History
Villanova University

Homelands
and Ancestors

The Nez Perce live in an area of North America called the Plateau, an area comprised of parts of what are now the states of Idaho, Oregon, and Washington, as well as adjacent sections of the Canadian province of British Columbia. The Nez Perce inhabit lands in the southeastern region of the Plateau, concentrated in western Idaho and nearby territory in eastern Oregon and Washington. They and their direct ancestors have lived in this region for at least 2,500 years.

The name *Nez Perce* comes from the French term for "pierced nose." The French used this name because they had heard that the Nez Perce had the custom of piercing their noses to wear ornaments made of dentalium shells. The people themselves have other names for their own group. The most common is *Ne-mee-poo,* sometimes also written as *Nimipuu* or *Nimipoo* by members of the contemporary tribe. In their own language, this name means

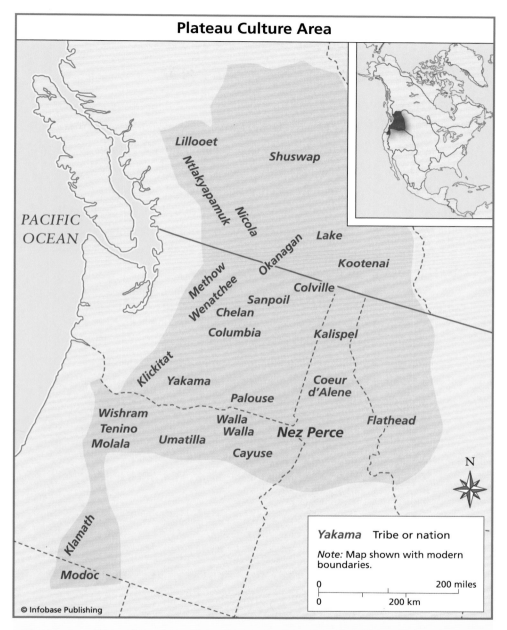

Plateau Culture Area

Lillooet

Shuswap

Ntlakyapamuk

Nicola

PACIFIC
OCEAN

Lake

Okanagan

Kootenai

Methow

Colville

Wenatchee

Sanpoil

Chelan

Columbia

Kalispel

Klickitat

Yakama

Coeur
d'Alene

Palouse

Wishram

Walla

Tenino

Walla

Flathead

Molala

Umatilla

Nez Perce

Cayuse

N

Yakama   Tribe or nation

Note: Map shown with modern
boundaries.

| 0 | | 200 miles |
| 0 | 200 km | |

Klamath

Modoc

© Infobase Publishing

The Plateau region of North America encompasses areas of Canada and the modern-day
states of Idaho, Montana, Washington, Oregon, and California. The Nez Perce primarily
inhabited the southeastern territory of the Plateau region, which includes parts of Idaho,
Oregon, and Washington.

the "real people" or "we, the people." Although the custom of nose piercing ended in the early nineteenth century, the term *Nez Perce* is still in general use.

ORIGIN STORIES

The Nez Perce have a sacred narrative that explains their origins. The story involves Coyote, a major figure in their spiritual beliefs. The story tells some of the exploits of Coyote and describes how he transformed some animals to their present shape. It also tells how Coyote released people who had been swallowed up by a huge monster. According to the narrative, as related by a contemporary Nez Perce storyteller for a collection by Haruo Aoki in his *Nez Perce Dictionary:*

> Coyote was just wandering downriver, and it was quiet around for a long time. Then he came up the river. And he learned that a Monster had swallowed everyone. He was all by himself. Then one who was left, whoever he was, said, "Monster swallowed them all now. And you too are to go there also." Now Coyote made plans. He went up this way here, high up, and he came to a place called Passasonam. Then Coyote made seven rawhide ropes there, quite long ones, and he tied himself to the Seven Devils mountains. Then he shouted to the Monster, "Let us inhale each other." Now the Monster heard him. Then it heard again, "Let's inhale each other."
>
> Now the Monster got ready, and breathed in. The wind moved Coyote, but he was held because he had himself tied down. Then Monster tried again, breathing more strongly; it was anxious to swallow Coyote. Now one rope broke. Then again Monster tried, and another rope broke, then all seven broke. Now Coyote was pulled and Monster took him in; Coyote was quickly pulled to Monster's mouth. "Now I swallowed you." He went on inside and first saw a rattlesnake acting vicious. Coyote said, "Why, what for are you being so vicious?" And he stepped on, kicked, and flattened its head. For this, rattlesnakes have flat heads. Then he walked into a grizzly bear and it acted vicious

toward Coyote. He said to the grizzly bear, "Why, what for are you being so vicious?" And he grabbed the grizzly bear's nose and flattened it with his hand. For this reason, grizzly bears have concave noses.

Then he saw so many people already starving to death. "Why are you making yourselves hungry, while this much meat is here?" The people said, "No, you are not going to do that. Monster will soon kill us all." Now he pulled out five agate knives. One he took out and he started cutting its heart. Then the knife broke. Then again he took out another and kept cutting like this, and all he pulled out. He broke the last knife as he was cutting. Now by a little bit the heart was attached, and Coyote pulled its heart loose. Then Monster dropped dead. Then Coyote cut Monster's meat for each, and he threw it to them saying, "Eat this!" Then the poor ones ate. Then Coyote told them, "Now we are going out." Then everyone came out of the Monster. Monster now lay dead.

Then Coyote cut it into pieces and threw them as he proceeded. He threw its leg to the eastern country of the Sioux, saying, "There they will be tall people." He threw each of its short arms to the south, and there they became short people. In this way, Coyote cut and distributed meat from various parts to each of the different people. But he forgot the Nez Perce people. Then he said, "I surely forgot these people who are living right here. I have not given them anything." Then he washed his hands, which were all bloody, and moistened the earth with the bloody water. And he told them, "Right here people will be brilliant and they will feel brave. They will be brilliant in everything."

The head of that Monster was up the river at Kooskia. And his body came down the river over the bluffs and all the way to Kamiah. Monster had such a body and down the river to the Udder Place. Its tail was down the river on the other side at the Lolo Creek. This was the size of that huge Monster. And Coyote killed it in that way. Then people were happy and became settled.

This story offers one explanation, in the rich poetic language of tradition, for the emergence of the Nez Perce and their neighbors on the Plateau and adjacent territory. Another type of explanation, this time in the contemporary language of science, provides evidence that aboriginal peoples have inhabited the Plateau region for at least 11,000 years.

EARLY WAYS OF LIVING

In former times, the people occupied land centering on three rivers in Idaho, Oregon, and Washington: the Snake, Clearwater, and Salmon rivers. Their territory encompassed varied features of rivers, deep canyons, and high plateaus. Temperatures and rates of precipitation varied as well, depending upon elevation. Because of these differences, people adjusted their living sites to changes in the seasonal availability of plant, fish, and animal resources. This lifestyle was an ancient one, dating back many centuries and indeed many millennia.

Early peoples were hunters and gatherers, dependent on the foods naturally available in their environment. This is a style of economic life called *foraging*. Resources available to the people included many species of fish, animals, and wild plants and fruits. At the earliest time of human settlement, the region was relatively dry in the winter and hot in the summer. Therefore, forests and their resources were less abundant than during later periods. Because of the variability in available resources, people were nomadic, moving frequently depending on food supplies. Their settlements were small and their dwellings were quickly built and easily dismantled.

The people used many types of tools and utensils to help them cut and grind their food. These included knives, pounding stones, scrapers, darts, anvils, and awls. Some of their tools and utensils were made of stone; others were made of animal bone or antler. For fishing, they used harpoons and nets weighted down with stones. They had needles made of bone that were probably used to sew clothing made of animal hides and possibly also to make coiled basketry. And they had beads made from soapstone that they obtained from their lands.

During a period beginning about 8,000 years ago, the Nez Perce refined their strategies for obtaining food. They hunted primarily deer, elk, rabbits, and birds, and collected mussels and caught many varieties of fish, especially salmon, sturgeon, and minnows. They also gathered many types of plants, fruits, and root crops. Later, about 5,000 years ago, rainfall increased in the Plateau region, encouraging the growth of forests and many types of plants. Plant growth helped lead to an increase in the number of animals, and also therefore the size of human populations that could exploit both plant and animal resources. During this same period, the number of fish, especially salmon, increased in the rivers. Fish would later form the basis of Nez Perce subsistence. Evidence remains of pits or small areas used for storing dried fish. This is an important innovation because it enabled people to amass more food, allowing them to stay in one place for longer periods of time.

Settlements then grew larger and somewhat more stable. Some of the dwellings were built partially in the ground and partially above the ground, a style called *semi-subterranean*. Some of the dwellings were circular while others were rectangular in shape. People seem to have used some of their houses seasonally, returning to them at different times of the year depending upon the available resources. Other houses may have been lived in all year-round. After the arrival of the horse, the Nez Perce used teepees during the summer.

Another significant finding from this period is evidence of trade among peoples. For example, archaeologists working at inland Plateau sites have found tools and ornaments made from obsidian from other regions and from dentalium and other shells from the Pacific Ocean. These finds firmly connect the Plateau region inhabited by Nez Perce ancestors to other peoples living to the south in the Great Basin and to western peoples living along the Pacific Coast in western Oregon and Washington. On the Plateau, trading was made easier by travel along the Columbia and

Fraser rivers and their tributaries. Trade networks later expanded northward into British Columbia.

Human populations declined considerably about 4,000 years ago, probably due to changes in climate and vegetation. Archaeologists believe that there are two possible ways that people adapted to these changes. One possibility is that people concentrated in the most favorable locations, abandoning smaller,

The early inhabitants of North America, and the Plateau region, learned how to make use of everything around them. Bone and different types of rocks and minerals could be shaped into weapons like knives or arrowheads, as well as household items such as needles or cooking utensils.

dispersed settlements. An alternative explanation is that people became more mobile, moving more frequently from place to place and therefore leaving fewer traces of their habitation. During this time, people began to exploit resources in higher elevations and possibly began to collect wild pine nuts for food.

The final prehistoric period began about 4,000 years ago and lasted until indigenous peoples of the Plateau began receiving influences from European cultures in the early eighteenth century. In the earliest phase of the prehistoric period, the temperatures on the Plateau decreased sharply and glacier formation advanced. In conjunction with heavier rainfall, forests expanded, supplying indigenous peoples with more food resources. One of the most important of these was the increase in salmon in the abundant rivers of the region. Greater reliability of available food led to stability of settlements since people could depend on local resources for extended periods of time. The previous preference for semi-subterranean houses reemerged as settlements became more permanent. Houses were larger and were dug deeper into the earth.

In addition to settled communities, people resided in small, temporary camps when fishing, hunting, or collecting roots, plants, and mussels—all major sources of food. These camps were located in the nearby river valleys, in order to have easy access to resources. Techniques for storing food also developed and became more frequently used. Houses contained pits for storage and sometimes ovens for processing food. The large storage pits within the houses enabled people to keep dried and preserved foods nearby. Researchers estimate that by about 2,000 years ago, ancestors of the modern Nez Perce relied on fish and mussels for about 50 percent of the protein in their diet.

The next series of climatic changes began about 2,000 years ago, resulting in warming and drying trends. New flood plains were formed along the Columbia and Snake rivers, especially in summer when heavy rainstorms flared up. Runoff from the storms helped support increased vegetation. With expanding plant growth, people traveled farther to procure new food sources, including into the higher elevations spreading out from river basins. Root crops were especially exploited. Technologies for processing root plants were developed and refined. In the southeastern regions of the Plateau, bison appear to have migrated into the lands from the adjacent western Plains. There is evidence of at least one site where large numbers of bison were killed and processed at the same time. Even so, despite the increased diversity of the food sources, salmon and root plants continued to dominate the regional diet.

Two significant innovations occurred during this period. There is evidence that people may have used fire in order to control and direct plant growth in regions upland from the rivers. In addition, people used bows and arrows for hunting, a technological advance that made hunting more efficient because hunters were able to shoot their prey from a far distance rather than having to be close to the animals.

Growth in food supplies led to changes in settlement patterns. Rather than living in many small settlements dispersed along the rivers, ancestors of the Nez Perce sometimes gathered together in large villages, some containing more than 100 dwellings. Significantly, the size of houses within a village often varied. Some of the larger houses measured more than 36 feet (12 meters) long. Variation in house size within a village has led some researchers to suggest that differences in relative wealth and social status had emerged by this time. The assumption here is that larger houses containing more goods and storage facilities for foods reflect higher social standing.

Finally, goods obtained from other peoples in other regions increased in number and variety. These included dentalium shells, beads made of shell, pipes for smoking, and many types of ornaments made of stone, whalebone, and animal antlers. There is evidence of differences among households in both the number and quality of trade goods that they had acquired. This evidence, too, supports assumptions that some people were wealthier and had higher status than others.

During this period, the importance of trade is reflected in the development of communities that were strategically located on trade routes. Some of these communities later expanded into large, centralized trading centers that became critical in the eighteenth and nineteenth centuries to the fortunes not only of indigenous peoples, but of European and American merchants as well.

The final set of changes in the cultures of the Nez Perce ancestors was in place by about 1,000 to 1,500 years ago. Variations in community size and settlement patterns are indicated by the growth of some villages. At the same time, population densities in other communities declined as the number of people in some concentrated settlements dispersed into many smaller communities living along the primary rivers of their territory, especially the Snake, Clearwater, and Salmon rivers. Semi-subterranean houses became less common, replaced by a preference for rectangular longhouses made of wooden poles covered with woven mats. In addition to findings of stone and bone tools and utensils, items made of perishable materials have been discovered. These include cordage, woven mats, and basketry. Within villages, there appears to be a disappearance of the social inequalities that were earlier indicated by differences in household size and the number of possessions a family held. This may reflect more equal social ethics.

These were the kinds of communities that existed in the eighteenth century when European and American merchants and travelers first encountered the Nez Perce. At that time, the Nez Perce were a prosperous people, exploiting their resources, traveling and trading with other groups, and strengthening their social values and their communities.

Community Life

The Nez Perce lived in a varied and abundant environment. Their aboriginal lands encompassed some 13 million acres (5.2 million hectares). Their territory included major rivers, small streams, deep canyons, hillsides, and plateaus. Each region of their territory contained many kinds of resources, enabling the people to have distinct varieties of foods in different seasons. Because of this diversity in food sources, the Nez Perce had a healthy and nutritious diet. The people lived in several kinds of settlements throughout the year so that they could travel to the places where resources were seasonally available. They depended upon one another in their family groups to help supply their food, clothing, and tools. They cooperated with one another to make decisions that affected the well-being and survival of their communities.

In *Journals of the Lewis and Clark Expedition,* Gary Moulton shares Meriwether Lewis's description of the Nez Perce territory

When Meriwether Lewis and William Clark first encountered the Nez Perce during their journey into the western United States, the explorers and their crew were met with generosity, guidance, and help. Without the invaluable knowledge of the Nez Perce, the Lewis and Clark expedition might not have survived the brutal terrain and climate of the Rocky Mountains.

that he visited in 1805 and 1806 during his exploratory expedition with William Clark:

> To its present inhabitants nature seems to have dealt with a liberal hand for she has distributed a great variety of esculent [succulent] plants over the face of the country which furnish them a plentiful store of provision; these are acquired with but little toil, when prepared after the method of the natives afford not only a nutritious but an agreeable food. Among the other roots those called by them "quawmash" [camas, a member of the lily family] and cows [cous] are esteemed the most agreeable and valuable as they are also the most abundant.

HUNTING AND GATHERING ON THE PLATEAU

The Nez Perce were foragers, using the resources naturally available in their environment. Foraging is an economic strategy that depends upon the cooperation of people in the household who work either together or separately to bring in varied resources. Foragers are also dependent upon the natural cycles of the earth. They need to have a great deal of knowledge about the seasonal growth of plants, the migration patterns of animals and birds, and the spawning cycles of fish. For the Nez Perce, this knowledge was learned and refined many centuries ago and then passed down from generation to generation. The Nez Perce and their direct ancestors have lived in the southern Plateau region for at least 2,500 years. Their connection to the specific lands that they occupy is intimate and sacred.

Economic tasks were carried out by men and women, sometimes working together and sometimes working separately. Women's work in supplying their families with food centered on gathering the many wild plants, roots, and fruits available in their territories. In total, about 135 species of edible plants were eaten. The most important of these to the Nez Perce diet were the root crops, especially camas, a member of the lily family. Other significant root plants included cous, bitterroot, and wild carrots and onions. Women used digging sticks made of wood to clear the ground and extract the roots. When explorers Lewis and Clark traveled among the Nez Perce in 1805 and 1806, they were told that root crops were the people's principal food. Indeed, researchers estimate that the roots and other plants that women collected contributed about 50 to 70 percent of the annual diet. The journals of Lewis and Clark describe the collection and cooking of various kinds of roots:

> The principal roots [camas] which they made use of for food are plenty. These prairies are covered with them. They are much like potatoes when cooked, and they have a curious way of cooking them. They have places made in the form of a small coal pit

and they heat stones in the pit. Then they put straw over the stones, then the water to raise steam. Then they put on large loaves of the pounded potatoes and 8 or 10 bushels of potatoes on at once. Then cover them with wet straw and earth. In that way they sweat them until they are cooked, and when they take them out, they pound some of them up fine and make them in loaves and cakes. [The Nez Perce] dry the cakes and string them on strings, in such a way that they would keep the year and handy to carry, any journey.

In addition to roots, women also collected many kinds of greens, shoots, mushrooms, fruits, and berries. Of the fruits and berries in their environment, gooseberries, huckleberries, currants, and chokecherries were the most significant. Women also gathered pine nuts and sunflowers seeds. If food supplies stored from the summer and fall dwindled by late in the winter, women gathered lichen and black moss to feed their families until spring plants became available. Moss, seeds, and nuts were generally roasted or boiled. They might be eaten plain or cooked in cakes or stews. Finally, people sometimes peeled the bark off pine trees and ate the inner layers, a sweet and nutritious food.

Nez Perce men were the primary fishers and hunters, although women participated in communal hunting and fishing endeavors. Men's work therefore accounted for about 30 to 50 percent of the annual diet. Most animal protein in the Nez Perce diet came from fish. Indeed, it is estimated that each person consumed an average of at least 500 pounds (225 kilograms) of fish per year. The principal fish sources were varieties of salmon, sturgeon, and lake trout, although other fish such as whitefish, minnows, suckers, and lampreys were also taken. All together, there were about 30 species of fish caught in the region.

The Nez Perce had a complex and diverse technology for catching fish. They used spears, harpoons, and hooks to catch fish individually, and they used dip nets and traps to catch large numbers of fish. Some of the nets measured about 325 feet

Nez Perce Recipes

Caroline James's collection of Nez Perce women's stories include statements from contemporary Nez Perce women recalling how their mothers and grandmothers described the foods that they prepared.

Then there's cous that you had to go out and dig among the hillsides. They'd peel the skin off them, wash them, and sun dry them. Then they look white. In the wintertime, a lot of these were served. Grandmother used to pound it to grains the size of oatmeal or cornmeal. Then, she'd put them into a round biscuit or make it into cereal. In the mornings, they'd have fresh cereal that's made out of cous. I used to watch my grandmother. She would grind the fresh cous, make a little ball, and take it in her hand and squeeze it. Her fingerprints would come. And then it was sun dried. She made a bunch of that, plus she made something that looked like bricks, a long bread called "o'ppah," and smoked them. It gave a particular flavor to it. Another bread was called "tsa'pu-khm-luct," and our grandmothers used to tell us, "That's a food that you have to eat in the springtime. Be thankful that you're living to eat these things." Way back then, they served it, and we are still serving it. I'm sorry to say, sometimes we don't have much time to go out and dig for those foods, but it's really delicious, and it's good for your health. That's the way we were told, so we try to tell that to our children, our grandchildren.

(100 meters) in length. People from several villages often cooperated in the construction of large traps and weirs (wooden fences built across streams), usually built on smaller streams that were tributaries of the major regional rivers. This work was overseen by men who were experts in rituals dedicated to fishing. They

The Nez Perce diet was based on hunting and gathering food. The men usually caught fish like salmon, sturgeon, and lake trout in special, wooden nets (*above*) while the women roasted or smoked the fish. Roots and plants, gathered with tools like a pickaxe (*above*), were seasonally available to the Nez Perce.

were also in charge of distributing the catch among all residents of the villages.

Of all the fish sought by the Nez Perce, the prize catch was salmon. Five varieties were sought, depending on the season and the sequence of spawning runs. When the rivers were thick with salmon, people paddled in canoes and caught the fish with spears or nets. They sometimes erected platforms on the rivers from which they could suspend their nets, enabling them to catch a large number of fish all at once. In Moulton's *Journals of the Lewis and Clark Expedition,* Clark gave the following description of fishing platforms: "[They build] a small stage or wharf consisting of sticks and projecting about 10 ft. [3 m] into the river and about

3 ft. [1 m] above the water. On the extremity of this, the fisherman stands with his scooping net. With these nets, they take the suckers and also the trout and the salmon."

Fish were prepared for eating by drying them in the sun or smoking them over a slow fire. Dried salmon was sometimes broiled or roasted. A majority of the catch was stored in large pits and storage baskets for use during the winter when the fresh supply of fish was exhausted.

Hunting also supplied significant sources of protein, although meat was not as important as fish in the Nez Perce diet. The major large animals sought included deer, elk, moose, mountain sheep, black bear, and grizzly bear. Smaller animals, especially rabbits, squirrels, and birds were also hunted. Bows and arrows were the most common weapons used in hunting. Hunters occasionally covered the tips of their arrows with rattlesnake poison to increase the likelihood of a kill. All able-bodied men and women participated together in communal hunting of deer and elk. There were several methods employed. The animals were sometimes lured into traps in open areas where hunters awaited and could then easily kill their prey. The people might attract the animals by erecting scarecrows or using decoys made of deer heads. Clark described one such decoy in his journals:

> These decoys are formed of the skin of the head and upper portion of the neck of that animal extended in the natural shape by means of a few little sticks placed within. The hunter, when he sees a deer, conceals himself and with his hand gives to the decoy the action of the deer at feed, and this induces the deer within arrowshot. In this mode the Indians near the woody country hunt on foot in such places where they cannot pursue the deer with horses, which is their favorite method when the grounds will permit.

Small animals and birds were most commonly taken with snares. When rabbits were plentiful, all men, women, and children in a village participated in catching them. They walked through the fields holding long nets to capture the animals. The most common birds taken were Canada geese, ducks, swans, and grouse.

Animal meat was prepared employing similar methods as those used for fish. The meat was frequently roasted or boiled. In order to boil meat, women put heated stones in large cooking baskets filled with water. They roasted the meat in ovens made of earth situated either inside or outside their dwellings. Women might also broil meat by attaching it to sticks suspended over an open fire.

According to the journals of Lewis and Clark, the Nez Perce occasionally resorted to eating horses if they had no other foods available, but this happened only in cases of extreme hunger. They refused, however, to eat dogs, no matter what the situation. American explorers, on the other hand, preferred to eat dogs rather than horsemeat when faced with dire circumstances.

Nez Perce subsistence activities followed a yearly cycle that went along with the cycles of the earth and its natural abundance. Gathering plants began in the early spring when the first root crops ripened in the lower river valleys. Communal hunts in search of deer and elk also took place in early spring, sometimes even using snowshoes when the snow was still deep. Soon, fishermen sought the first salmon as the fish began their spawning runs on the Snake and Columbia rivers.

Crucial to the spring cycle were the rituals performed to welcome the arrival of the first roots and the first salmon in the Nez Perce environment. The ceremonies were led by specialists who recited prayers in honor of the plants and fish upon which the people depended for their survival. The Nez Perce believed that these rituals pleased the spirit guardians of the plants and fish. If the rituals were not performed properly, the spirit guardians would withhold their bounty and the people would suffer.

Later, as summer arrived, plants, fish, and animals became more abundant and were easily gathered or caught in all regions of the territory. People would often move to campsites in the higher elevations in order to procure these resources. As fall and winter approached, the majority of foods taken were prepared for winter storage so that people would have enough to eat when resources were scarce. At that time, people moved back to their winter villages near the rivers, where temperatures were milder than they were at higher elevations.

In addition to consuming plants, fish, and animals as food, the Nez Perce used these resources in their tools, utensils, and clothing. In particular, most clothing was made of animal hides, especially from deer and elk. Men wore long shirts made of deer or elk skin, leggings, and breechcloths. They wore short moccasins on their feet. Women's clothing consisted of dresses made of deer or elk skin and knee-length moccasins. They also wore caps made of woven fibers. In cold weather, people wore buckskin gloves to protect their hands.

Men and women decorated their faces with painted designs. The paint was made with dyes obtained from plants and berries. Clothing was also decorated with paint, as well as with porcupine quills and beads made of shell and bone. Women's dresses were decorated with elk teeth and shells originating in the Pacific Ocean that were obtained through trade networks.

NEZ PERCE SETTLEMENTS

The Nez Perce lived in distinct types of settlements during different seasons. During the winter, they resided in stable villages situated along the banks of the rivers and streams in their territory. These villages varied in size. Some contained only a few dwellings, while others contained more than a hundred. In the summer, they lived in smaller camps located in the upland regions where they moved temporarily to exploit seasonally available resources. In 1800, there were 70 permanent villages, each populated by between 30 and 200 people, depending on the season. At that time, there were a total of 300 living sites, including the smaller camps.

The Nez Perce built two different types of structures to house themselves: the conical, tipi shelter in the summer and the longhouse (*above*) for the cooler seasons. Similar to other Native American longhouses, the Nez Perce Longhouse could serve as a home for approximately 30 families.

The structures that the Nez Perce erected in the villages and summer camps differed. The largest houses were those used during the winter. They were of the "longhouse" design: rectangular in shape, made of a wooden frame, and covered with woven mats and straw. These houses varied in size. The largest might measure 100 to 150 feet (30 to 45 m) in length. In his journals, Lewis offered a description of a large dwelling:

> It is 156 feet long and about 15 wide [47.5 m by 4.5 m], built of mats and straw. In the form of the roof of the house having a number of small doors on each side, it is closed at the ends and without divisions in the intermediate space, this lodge contained at least 30 families. Their fires are kindled in a row in the

center of the house and about 10 feet [3 m] apart. All the lodges of these people are formed in this manner.

Summer lodges erected in temporary fishing and hunting camps were sometimes built according to the same design, but were smaller and accommodated fewer families. Some summer lodges were conical in shape, framed by wooden poles covered with hides or mats.

In addition to household dwellings, the Nez Perce had two types of structures for specialized uses. They had sweat lodges that people entered in order to purify their bodies, either as part of ceremonial activities or for cleansing and health purposes. These lodges were built partially underground. Stones were first heated in fires and then placed in the lodge through a hole in the top. People then threw hot water on the stones in order to create more heat and steam. Once the lodge was prepared, participants entered through the small hole on the top. The sweat lodge and its use was described by Clark in his journals:

> At this place I saw a curious sweat house underground with a small hole at the top to pass in or throw in the hot stones, which those inside threw on as much water as to create the temperature of heat they wished. . . . The men went early to a sweat house, built a large fire and put in a large quantity of small stones and heated them red-hot, then put them in some water in the sweat hole which was prepared for that purpose and only a hole big enough to get in one at a time. About twelve at once got in to the hole until they sweat and went in the water and bathed themselves. Then in the hole again and bathed themselves in that way for about two hours.

Nez Perce villages also had menstrual lodges that girls and women resided in during their menstrual periods. These structures were built with the same materials as longhouses, but were much smaller. They were positioned close to the main dwellings.

FAMILIES AND HOUSEHOLDS

Nez Perce households were made up of families who cooperated with each other in order to obtain supplies of foods and other goods, to secure their shelters, to socialize their children, and to give one another emotional support. The Nez Perce traced descent through both women and men. That is, people considered themselves related to other people through their mothers and through their fathers. This is a system of kinship called "bilateral." (*Bi* means "two" and *lateral* means "sides.") People formed informal groupings of relatives called *kindreds.* These consisted of all people related to one another through their mothers and fathers. People belonging to a kindred showed hospitality and generosity to one another. In addition, they owed each other assistance in times of need. They also supported each other in conflicts with others, and were allies in political or military endeavors.

Kinship and descent were the basis of the most important social bonds among people. Marriage also formed critical social bonds, not only between the married couple but among their relatives as well. Nez Perce rules prohibited marriage between any known relatives, whether close or distant. The bonds between families created by marriage ideally continued even after the death of one spouse. For example, if a husband died, one of his brothers might marry the widow (a pattern called the *levirate*). Similarly, if a wife died, one of her sisters was likely to take her place as the wife of the widower (a practice called the *sororate*). The purpose of these customs was to maintain alliances between families that had been established with the initial marriage.

Nez Perce households usually consisted of more than one nuclear family (meaning a set of parents and their children). The extended families making up this arrangement could be formed through multiple generations or through combinations of two or more nuclear families. For example, an extended household might consist of an elderly couple, their unmarried children and their married children, and the families of these children. Also, several siblings or cousins and their families could combine to form an extended household.

Although the rules for residence after marriage were flexible, the ideal pattern was for a newly married couple to live in the husband's household. Since men's work required cooperation in fishing and hunting expeditions, it made sense for men to live with their relatives. However, actual residence patterns showed a great deal of variation. Indeed, many couples moved back and forth at various times between the relatives of the husband and those of the wife. Specific choices might be made on the basis of available resources, the composition of already existing households, and personal preferences.

Younger couples and individuals, in particular, tended to be quite mobile. They might change their residence when convenient and could always depend on the hospitality of their relatives. As people grew older, they tended to have more stable living arrangements. Elderly couples were especially likely to live permanently in one place, attracting younger relatives for their knowledge, experience, and good reputation. Indeed, grandparents played a central role in the care and socialization of their grandchildren. The bond between these generations was perhaps the most affectionate of all kin relationships.

Family and community relationships were based on ethics of sharing and giving. In the words of a contemporary Nez Perce woman included in Caroline James's collection:

> Indians were a really close-knit family. Everybody helped each other then. I can remember when living by the river, we never went anyplace or traveled that much, but we were in the area where people would come by our place, and our place was a convenient stopping place, so that older people were coming through, sometimes they would stop overnight, or sometimes they would stop and visit for a while, and Mom would say, "Go out there and pick some cherries for them." Get some cantaloupes, tomatoes, whatever we had, and we would give it to them. Giving was a strong part of our culture.

COMMUNITY LEADERSHIP

Nez Perce society was based on ethics of equality. All people were understood to have equal rights to resources and to opportunities for prestige and respect. Everyone's work and contributions to their households were valued. Although men and women might have somewhat different roles in their families and communities, they had equal status and their opinions were equally valued. These ethics, taken together, are called *egalitarian* principles. In practice, of course, some people were more respected by community members than others because of their good judgment, wisdom, success, and favored personalities. Seniority, for example, gave an individual some degree of influence and respect because a person's life experiences gave him or her extra knowledge and insight.

Each Nez Perce winter village had a leader, or headman, selected by members of the village council who were themselves the heads of the extended families who resided there. The council usually chose the eldest family leader in that settlement as the headman, but the eldest might be overlooked in favor of another candidate deemed more fitting on the basis of his knowledge, good judgment, success, and valued personality traits. The intelligence, experience, and personality of a candidate's wife was also taken into account because a leader's wife was often one of his trusted advisers. In addition, leaders were usually assisted by younger men. The headman acted as a spokesman for his village, settled disputes among members of his village, and promoted the well-being and security of the community. Even though leaders were respected, they very much led by influence and example, and could not force their will on others.

Although each Nez Perce village was autonomous and independent, villages that were located along the same stream or tributary considered themselves members of a unit called a *band*. Bands had councils made up of each village's leaders. Like villages, band councils selected a leader, usually the person who was the leader of the largest village in that grouping. Bands cooperated in some economic pursuits, but in particular they joined forces for the defense of their member villages. Several bands might similarly be joined into a larger grouping called a *composite band*. Each composite band had a council composed of the leaders of the various bands. Prominent community leaders and warriors were also members of these councils.

Disputes that occurred in Nez Perce communities were settled in various ways. Conflicts among members of a family grouping were negotiated by the leader, in consultation with elder men and women who had good reputations for their sound judgment and personal charisma. If disputes arose between members of different families within a village, the village leader and council had a role to play in helping to solve the problem, but their influence was personal rather than structural. That is, they could not impose a solution, but instead could only offer advice and hope that their reputations added weight to their opinions. Village councils only intervened in rare occasions when, for example, specific individuals were thought by the community to be unredeemable troublemakers. In those cases, the offenders might be exiled from the community.

In addition to village and band leaders, known as peace chiefs, warriors who excelled in the defense of their communities were recognized for their courage and bravery. These men sometimes served as assistants to the peace leaders but their roles were separate. War chiefs could organize expeditions against their enemies and were in charge of home defense. The men who accompanied them did so voluntarily because they approved of the war chief's plans. Although prestige came to men who took part in war, no one was forced to participate.

Village and band councils held periodic meetings to discuss issues relevant to their groups. At these meetings, headmen and leaders solicited the opinions of members of their communities before taking any actions. All men and women in the community could participate and voice their opinions. Leaders could not act alone; they could only act after having secured support from their constituents. Indeed, the strength of Nez Perce communities was based on the values and ethics of equality, consideration of public opinion, and respect for everyone.

These values were also reflected in Nez Perce religious beliefs and practices. To them, the spirit world could be contacted for aid and support. They honored spirit beings with prayers and rituals based on their own social ethics of generosity.

Spirits and Powers

The Nez Perce world is inhabited by many kinds of beings. These include humans, plants, animals, and spirits. In their system of belief, the Nez Perce must establish special relationships with all of these beings. They are expected to cooperate with other people in establishing families and communities, and to show respect to the plants and animals upon which they depend for survival. Finally, they must honor the spirits who protect them, give them knowledge, and help them survive and succeed.

To the Nez Perce, the world is filled with a spiritual essence or power that inhabits all living creatures, including people, animals, plants, and the earth itself. Natural entities and forces such as celestial bodies, mountains, rivers, winds, and thunder also contain spirit essence. Going along with their egalitarian ethics, the Nez Perce believe that everyone can have access to spirit powers and can make direct contact with the spirit world. People can acquire spirit powers through prayer, song, and dance. In addition, spirit powers sometimes come spontaneously to people in dreams and visions. Participation in rituals is a way of both obtaining and enacting special knowledge and power.

Although everyone has access to spirit power in principle, in practice some people gain more knowledge and power than others. Success in any endeavor is a demonstration of spirit power, while failure and misfortune are indications that a person lacks these powers. A man or woman who is able to obtain a great deal of spirit power may become a religious specialist called a *shaman*. Such people often have extraordinary abilities and insights. They are thought to be able to foretell the future, locate game and other food sources, and intervene in conflicts. They can interpret spiritual omens seen by people in dreams or visions. Shaman may also be called on to diagnose and cure diseases because of their knowledge of the medicinal qualities of plants and animals and their expertise in the rituals that treat illnesses. Indeed, this is one of their most important functions. Finally, shaman have roles to play in community and individual ceremonies.

RITES OF PASSAGE

Rites of passage are ceremonies that mark transitions from one stage of life to another. Major stages in the lifecycle that are marked by rituals include birth, coming of age (when a person is considered an adult), marriage, and death. Some of the Nez Perce rites of passage are no longer performed today, although others may be practiced by some members of the contemporary community.

Before a baby was born, Nez Perce mothers observed certain procedures in order to ensure a safe delivery and protect the baby's health. An expectant mother engaged in exercise, took hot and cold baths, and drank teas made with medicinal herbs. She refrained from touching or looking at people or animals who were deformed because it was feared that if she did so, her baby would also be deformed or sickly. In addition, she did not tie knots in clothing, mats, or baskets, believing that this would prevent obstructions in the delivery that would cause harm to herself or the baby.

When a baby was due, the mother retired to a small lodge, accompanied by her mother, other female relatives, and a midwife. A contemporary Nez Perce woman, quoted in James's collection, described a small hole that was dug in the ground so that "all of the blood and the afterbirth and everything was buried in this hole after the child was born." In cases of a difficult delivery, a ritual specialist might be called in to assist the birth. The specialist used medicinal herbs, massage, and sacred songs and rituals that were received from spirit helpers. As soon as a baby was born, its head and feet were massaged to form them into the desired shape. The umbilical cord was cut and placed in a special container made of animal hide, which was then attached to the baby's cradleboard. The cord was considered a vital part of one's being, and would thus remain with the baby as he or she grew. Once these rituals were completed, feasts were held and gifts were given by relatives in honor of the mother and baby.

Names for the baby were selected from those of successful, prominent, and respected ancestors, because it was thought that the same qualities associated with these names would then develop in the new child. People also had nicknames by which they were generally known, and could take new names at any point in their lives. These names might reflect significant events, accomplishments, and personality traits.

The next transition that was marked by ritual occurred when a child made his or her first major contribution to the family subsistence efforts. When a girl first successfully dug up root crops or a boy made his first catch of a fish or animal, a ceremony was held in his or her honor. These ceremonies were accompanied by feasts and speeches praising the child. A child's future was deemed especially favored if a renowned hunter or a skilled gatherer ate

The Nez Perce honors the transition from adolescence to adulthood with the first rites passage and ceremony, a tradition that is still practiced. Young men and women are prepared and encouraged to spend time in sweat lodges, avoid sleep, and even take cold baths in order to help them concentrate on finding their spirit helpers. Above, a group of Nez Perce men, women, and children dressed in traditional clothing during a first rites ceremony in Idaho.

the child's first food offering. Rituals such as these typically took place when children were about six years old.

Among the most significant personal ceremonies were those that marked a young person's passage to adulthood. Sometime during adolescence, boys and girls sought their individual spirit helpers, called *tutelary spirits*. Parents encouraged their children to seek these spirit powers so that the child would have lifelong protection. After several years of training, the seekers prepared themselves through cleansing and purification in sweat lodges.

Once prepared, the young person went into the woods or to a mountaintop, guided by parents or close relatives, in order to seek his or her tutelary spirit. The person was then left alone and dedicated themselves to the task by fasting, not sleeping, taking cold baths if possible, and concentrating their minds on spiritual matters. If successful, a spirit might appear to the seeker and give them a special song that they could sing when summoning the aid of their helper. Spirits appeared in human form, although they might have qualities of animals as well. The seeker sometimes also found a special object such as an unusually shaped stone, bird feather, or animal tooth that offered spiritual protection. Some people sought visions several times, acquiring additional powers. People who failed to receive visionary help in their first attempt usually went out again in order to achieve the desired result. Success in life was often attributed to the power of one's spirit helpers, while failures might result from the absence of such assistance.

The objects that a person might find on his or her vision quest were kept together in a sacred bundle. These objects were occasionally taken out and purified so that their powers would remain strong. The specific nature of one's powers was not always immediately clear. People might go to a shaman who could help them understand how to use their powers effectively.

In addition to visionary quests, young girls participated in special rituals at the time of their first menstruation. When menarche occurred, the girl left her usual abode and went to a special lodge constructed nearby. The girl was joined there by her mother and several older female relatives. She stayed in the lodge all day but could go out in the evenings for short periods of time. She ate food cooked on a fire separate from that of the rest of her family, and she was given a carved scratching stick to use so that she did not touch her body if she needed to scratch an itch. This was deemed a very special and powerful time in a girl's life. The power that she had could affect others, particularly men. As noted by a Nez

Perce woman in James's collection, for this reason, a girl's menstrual blood was buried in a hole in the lodge so "that their power wouldn't affect any of the men." Lewis offered further detail in his journal of his visits to the Nez Perce: "The men are not permitted to approach this lodge within a certain distance and if they have anything to convey to the occupants, they stand at the distance of 50 or 60 paces and throw it towards them as far as they can and retire."

The girl's separation lasted about one week. Then, a public ceremony was held to welcome her into her community as an adult woman, ready for marriage. She was given new clothing and many gifts by her relatives and friends.

Marriages among the Nez Perce were celebrated primarily through feasting and exchanges of gifts between the families of the bride and groom. First marriages were generally arranged by the heads of the respective families. An elder female relative of the prospective groom began marriage negotiations once the family had decided that the choice was appropriate, usually taking into account the reputation and social standing of both the prospective spouse and his or her family. If the woman's family agreed, the couple began to visit with each other and the families would meet periodically for feasting. Then, if the union seemed favorable, the couple started to live together.

If all went well, the ceremonial exchange of gifts began. The groom's family first brought gifts to the bride's kin, and then the bride's family reciprocated. James's collection shares a contemporary Nez Perce woman's recollection of the tradition:

> Fish, meat, and related foods are usually served at the first trade, the men's sphere. Roots, berries, and such are represented at the second, the women's trade. Before each occasion, ten women are chosen by and from each side to conduct the trade. They kneel in two facing lines, with their goods on the floor in front of them. A leader of the host's line commences, handing a first gift to the opposite guests. The guest reciprocates, and so on.

The symbolism of men's and women's roles was also reflected by the foods served when each group hosted the feasts. Women's families served varieties of roots while men's relatives served meat. At the end of the second exchange of gifts and foods, the couple was deemed married.

Most marriages were stable, but in the event of an unhappy relationship, either spouse could initiate divorce simply by taking their belongings and leaving the household. Although divorce did not carry any social stigma, most couples remained together because they had gotten to know each other well before the marriage was finalized. Also, families of the spouses tended to discourage separation, since the two families had become allies through the union of their children.

The final stage of life, marked by solemn ceremony, was death. News of a person's death was announced throughout the village by a special crier. Female relatives of the deceased began to wail, a signal that other relatives and friends heeded as they gathered around the body. The deceased was given a ritual bath and a new set of clothing. His or her face was decorated with red paint. Then, the next day, the deceased was wrapped in a robe and taken to burial on a slope overlooking the village, with the place marked by a wooden stake. People avoided the spot afterwards.

Some possessions were buried with the deceased, as well, in order to accompany them in the afterlife. Grave goods were symbolic of the roles and interests of the deceased. For example, men might be buried with their fishing or hunting gear or with weapons of war, while women were buried with their cooking baskets, utensils, and beaded bags. Horses owned by the deceased might be sacrificed at the site of the grave. Indeed, Clark reported observing that 28 horses were sacrificed during the death rituals for a wife of one of the Nez Perce leaders whom he met on his expedition.

The tutelary spirits that a person had acquired during his or her lifetime departed at death. However, sometimes the spirit

Like many other cultures, the Nez Perce commemorates the most important passages in life—birth, adulthood, marriage, and death—with tradition and ceremony. Because it is believed that people continue on with their everyday activities after they have passed away, the deceased are usually buried with the items they used most often in their lives. Above, a funeral ceremony is performed on the Colville Indian Reservation in Washington.

might appear to one of the deceased's relatives in a dream, thus indicating that it wanted to remain nearby.

When the burial was completed, relatives of the person who had passed away hosted a ceremonial feast for members of the community. At that time, the deceased's possessions were distributed to friends and relatives according to wishes that the deceased had previously expressed. In some cases, relatives contributed additional gifts to be distributed in the person's honor. It was deemed crucial that the funerary practices be conducted in the proper manner in order to show respect. These rituals freed the individual's soul and allowed it to have a successful journey to the afterworld. To the Nez Perce, the afterworld was like the present world. People continued the same types of activities in the afterlife as they had done while living.

Following a death, close relatives of the deceased went into a period of mourning that lasted one year. During this time, a surviving spouse had to keep his or her hair short, wear old clothing, and refrain from laughing or seeming to be happy. According to a Nez Perce woman quoted in James's collection, whenever a surviving spouse cut or combed his or her hair, they "collect their hair in a pouch, don't throw it away. They bury it, or when they die it went with them." The name of the deceased was never spoken. In some cases, his or her household furnishings and even the house itself might be abandoned or destroyed. At the end of the year of mourning, a surviving spouse was given a new set of clothing and could then remarry.

THE WINTER TUTELARY SPIRIT DANCE

A major Nez Perce ceremony involved practices that honored and demonstrated people's tutelary spirits. These ceremonies have recently been revived by some members of the Nez Perce community. The Spirit Dance took place every winter, lasting from 5 to 10 days. During this period, young people who had that year received their tutelary spirits in a vision quest celebrated their success. They sang the song or songs given to them in their visions or dreams. Then anyone in the community who wished to do so could also sing their songs and honor their spirit helpers. Finally, shamans demonstrated their powers, singing their sacred songs and performing dances given to them by their tutelary spirits. In addition, shamans might demonstrate their extraordinary powers to locate lost objects, foretell the future, and control the weather by causing thunderstorms.

Winter dances were also occasions for the transfer of power from people with stronger powers to those with weaker ones. The

Winter Spirit Dances

The Winter Spirit Dances were among the most dramatic of all Nez Perce rituals. Here, an 80-year-old woman describes these rituals in a collection of women's voices compiled by Caroline James:

> There was a religious ceremony that involved medicine men and medicine women who were very successful in their "weyekin" Spirit. They would participate in their "weyik wecit" or guardian spirit dance. These dances always took place in the winter season in the longhouses. These dances were arranged by the medicine people to honor their spirits. Giftgiving was a part of this religious ceremony by the medicine people who host this ceremony. A feast would be given. In the evening, they dressed in their ceremonial, colorful, and decorated clothing. They would start dancing and they danced the whole night. During the dances, the medicine people would make symbols like a feather or fur and wave them. These symbols were related to their spirits. While dancing, they revealed their identified spirits, and they sang their sacred songs that had been given or taught by their "weyekin" spirits.
>
> Sometimes an individual would be recognized as more powerful than the rest of the medicine people. If there was one more powerful than that person, then while dancing they would touch others. And, all of a sudden, the person touched would fall on the floor or go into a trance. Then, that most powerful would touch them and kind of make them straight. All these medicine people must dance and sing their songs to strengthen themselves.

transfer usually involved some sort of payment for the service. During the ritual, the stronger person carried the weaker one around the dance area. Eventually, the weaker person entered a trance state, a state of altered consciousness during which he or she received powers from the stronger person. As a result of the exposure to strong power, the recipient often became ill and was subsequently cured in a ritual treatment led by a shaman.

Winter dances also helped strengthen communities and allegiances with nearby villages. Each year, the winter dance was sponsored by the headman of a band, a grouping of neighboring villages. The headman and his relatives were responsible for hosting the dance and for providing the feasts that accompanied the ritual. The ceremony itself was directed by one or more shamans who were allies of the sponsoring headman. At the end of the winter dance, the host gave gifts to all of the participants. These gifts included food, tools and utensils, clothing, and ornaments. The host amassed the necessary gifts through his own labor and that of his relatives. Their generosity helped to enhance their collective prestige.

ILLNESS AND HEALING

Nez Perce concepts of illness and healing center on notions of harmony and balance. People believe that health is a state of balance between people and their social and spiritual environments. In order to remain healthy, people should maintain good relationships with others, be cooperative, helpful, and generous. People also should seek and obtain tutelary spirits whose powers protect one's health and life. They should honor all of the spirit beings by performing rituals in their honor and avoiding behavior that offends them.

Health was also said to be maintained with the use of medicinal plants and by acts of cleansing and purification. People took sweat baths prior to participating in rituals and as an occasional practice to cleanse their bodies and minds. As part of a daily regimen for health, people took cold baths in the waters of nearby rivers in every season of the year. People also drank teas made of herbs and plants for a variety of digestive problems. Tobacco was burned and smoked as a cleanser and as a mode of communication with the spirit world.

No matter how careful a person might be, everyone occasionally gets sick. Among the Nez Perce, there were two types of specialists to treat the ill. Some men and women had vast knowledge of the medicinal qualities of plants and animals in their environment. Indeed, there were more than 120 species of medicinal plants known and used by the Nez Perce. Medicinal specialists could diagnose and treat a wide array of problems, including colds, coughs, indigestion, headaches, nausea, swellings, and various internal pains. They gave patients doses of medicines, used massage treatments, and could set broken bones. Their practice also had a spiritual component, because whenever they collected plant specimens they had to recite prayers of thanks to honor the spirit sources of these medicines in order for the remedies to be effective.

If medicinal treatment alone did not succeed in curing the patient, a shaman could perform rituals after determining that there was a spiritual cause for the ailment. The most common type of spiritual cause was a curse sent to the patient either by a spirit as a punishment for some misbehavior, or by a human being acting out of ill will. The curse showed itself as an object or substance that appeared suddenly within a person's body. The shaman began the ceremony by singing the songs that he or she had received from tutelary spirits. Next, the shaman needed to find the location of the curse. He or she might then extract it by using a sucking horn made from animal bone. Some shaman have the power to extract an ailment by touching the spot with their index finger. Especially powerful shaman might be able to extract the curse simply by concentrating their minds on the task.

In addition to their spiritual powers, in order to be respected, shaman had to act in ways that demonstrated their worthiness. A contemporary Nez Perce observer, included in James's collection, commented on the behavior of a medicine woman or shaman:

> A medicine woman had to be really careful what, and how she spoke to people, how she treated people. She wasn't supposed to

When a sick or injured person did not respond to medical treatments, the Nez Perce often turned to shamans. These medicine men and women conducted rituals that determined the spiritual reasons and the source of a person's suffering, as well as a cure.

get angry at anyone. She had to keep her mind clean, keep her home clean, keep her family with strict rules what to live by so that her children also knew that she was supposed to be that way. She kept herself clean, kind to people, willing to help when they needed help. She had to be generous. She had to be able to share what she had, to show the younger generation what they should be like.

The Nez Perce believed that nearly anyone could cause illness and misfortune to others by purposely thinking evil thoughts, or with simply a passing wish in reaction to some offense or slight committed by the victim. However, some people engaged in more elaborate practices to harm others. Shamans themselves might be suspected of causing harm, since they controlled and could use more powerful spiritual sources. As a result, care needed to be taken to avoid offending other people. In these ways, belief in the ability of people to cause harm encouraged proper behavior, helpfulness, cooperation, and respect for members of one's family and community.

SACRED NARRATIVES

Like all peoples throughout the world, the Nez Perce have stories that they tell about their origins and how Earth and all living creatures got to be the way they are. The stories also impart lessons and morals, providing blueprints for proper behavior by relating the good things that happen to people who act properly and the bad consequences that occur when people do not follow social and spiritual rules. Nez Perce ethical principles are communicated through stories about people or animals who are generous and kind, helpful to their relatives and neighbors, and courageous in the face of hardship. The stories champion people or animals who protect their group and promote the survival of all. In contrast, some stories demonstrate the harm that can befall people if they are stingy, greedy, and malicious.

Nez Perce narratives also teach children about their own social and physical geography. The stories are usually set in a specific locale, such as by a specific river, near a local mountaintop, or any other familiar geographical feature. As children hear these stories, they absorb knowledge of their surroundings and of the sites that are important in their history. Narratives may relate events that involve other peoples, close or distant neighbors of the Nez Perce. These stories help teach children about the relationships that their group has with others.

Winter was the time when stories were told, both during ritual occasions such as the tutelary spirit dance and during evenings spent at home. Elders were the primary storytellers. Grandmothers and grandfathers instructed and entertained their grandchildren and other youngsters by reciting the exploits of legendary characters. Principal among these is Coyote.

Coyote is a trickster figure, a character who has both positive and negative human traits. He is fearless, daring, and generous, but he is also envious, rude, selfish, and vain. Coyote's adventures and mishaps helped to transform the physical environment in which the Nez Perce live and the characteristic features of animals and plants. The stories involving Coyote are also imaginative, exciting, and humorous, providing welcome entertainment on cold, dark winter evenings.

The Nez Perce say that the stories took place long before even prehistoric times. The adventures of Coyote and of all the spirit beings who inhabit Earth occurred before human beings came to be. The world of the narratives ended just as people arrived on the scene, but according to the tales this sacred world continues to influence people's lives. People strive to make contact with this world by acquiring and summoning their tutelary spirits so that they can have protection and aid to ensure their survival and good fortune.

Nez Perce elders would soon have a new story to tell. They would tell of interactions with strangers who began entering their territory in the early eighteenth century. These interactions would lead to far-reaching life changes.

Strangers Bearing New Goods

The Nez Perce lived in relative stability for hundreds of years, obtaining resources from the land and interacting with their neighbors in trade, intermarriage, and social and ritual occasions. But unbeknownst to them, strangers began appearing in far-distant regions of the continent by the early sixteenth century. The effects of the actions and policies of these strangers were not felt by the Nez Perce until the early eighteenth century, about 200 years after the Europeans made their first landfall in North America. At first, the Nez Perce prospered from contact with Europeans. They obtained goods that benefited them and they enriched themselves through widening networks of trade. Later, however, the results of contact proved disastrous as Nez Perce lands were taken, as their population declined from disease, and as they came under the authority of foreign governments.

ACQUIRING HORSES

The first material change for the Nez Perce was a thoroughly positive one: They acquired horses through trade with other indigenous peoples who themselves had obtained the animals from Spanish traders and settlers in what later became known as the American Southwest. This process began in the early eighteenth century, probably around 1720. Horses revolutionized Nez Perce economies and ways of living in several respects. People on horseback were able to expand their resource base, traveling far distances to areas abundant in roots and other plants and to follow animals that they hunted.

People could also use horses to carry back plants that they gathered or the hides and meat of animals that they killed. Horses

Introduced to North America through Spanish colonization, the horse changed traditional Native American economies and traditions. After trading with eastern Native American tribes, the Nez Perce acquired their first horses and quickly adapted the travois, a sled used for transporting heavy loads, to use with their new animals (*above*).

did not carry loads directly on their backs, but instead pulled loads that were piled on a structure called a *travois*. Travois were constructed of two poles tied together at one end, opening into a V at the other end. A hide was stretched across the poles so that goods of all kinds could be placed on top of it. The top end of the travois was tied to the horse's sides so that it dragged along the ground. This same type of structure was previously pulled by dogs before the acquisition of horses, but dogs could not pull as large or heavy loads as could horses. Since the Nez Perce moved seasonally from place to place to exploit resources in their varied environments, it was senseless to amass more clothing, implements, and foods than could be easily transported. Once people acquired horses, they could use the animals to carry heavy burdens.

In addition to their usefulness in subsistence activities, horses enabled Nez Perce warriors to travel further distances in shorter periods of time to confront their enemies. They could make rapid attacks and retreat quickly to their own lands. Prowess in warfare became an important ingredient in a man's social prestige. Especially daring and successful warriors could become leaders in their villages and bands.

Finally, within Nez Perce communities, the number of horses that an individual or family owned became a significant measure of wealth and status. As a group, the Nez Perce owned more horses than any other peoples in the Plateau region. They were known as skilled horsemen and horsewomen. They also concentrated on breeding their horses for qualities of speed, strength, and endurance, a practice that was uncommon in Native America. Their horses were among the finest on the continent.

TRADE WITH OTHER NATIVE NATIONS

During the second half of the eighteenth century, the Nez Perce continued to acquire and breed more horses, adding to their reputation and to their ability to exploit resources and defend their territories. They also continued to actively participate in intertribal trade that had been well-established hundreds of years earlier. Trade routes extended from the Pacific Coast, inland along the Columbia River and its numerous tributaries, and through the prairies and plains of the Upper Northwest. The trading season lasted from late spring until late in the summer.

There were several key centers of intertribal trade to which the Nez Perce had regular access. The most important was the Dalles commercial center, located on the Columbia River just east of the Cascade Mountain range in what is now northern Oregon. There, men and women traders from the coastal regions in western Oregon, Washington, and British Columbia brought marine shells, whale oil and blubber. People from the western regions of the Plateau brought animal skins, woven mats, and breads made from roots. From the southern Plateau, the Nez Perce and their neighbors brought horses, camas roots, animal hides, and buffalo robes. The Nez Perce obtained buffalo robes both from their own forays into the plains of Montana and from their trade with other indigenous groups, especially the Flathead.

The Nez Perce sought many types of goods in these exchanges, especially marine shell beads and a product known as salmon pemmican that was produced by people living in villages near the Dalles along the Columbia River basin. Salmon pemmican was made of dried salmon pounded into a paste and then kept in baskets lined with salmon skins. This food could then be stored and eaten in later seasons. Researchers now estimate that about one million pounds of salmon pemmican was produced and traded each year.

In addition to trading at the Dalles, Nez Perce traders participated in other commercial centers located in eastern Oregon at the Grande Ronde and at Celilo Falls, in eastern Washington at Kettle Falls, and at other sites in the area. In all of these locations, indigenous men and women from many regions exchanged goods, met and socialized with each other, found marriage partners, and learned each other's stories. Although many languages were spoken at these trading centers, and people were often bilingual or multilingual, the Nez Perce language began to be used by other peoples in trading interactions. This was yet another reflection of the dominance that the Nez Perce exerted in their region.

For the Nez Perce and other indigenous peoples, commerce was not merely an economic exchange. Trade was embedded in social networks and social relationships. People established stable partnerships with particular individuals who they sought out time after time at the same trading centers. Trade itself was viewed as an exchange of gifts of equal value, not as a context for making a profit. If people did not know each other well, then some bargaining might take place, but eventually people who traded regularly with one another established social relations as well.

For example, the following is a description of an encounter between Nez Perce and Spokane traders in Washington, as recorded in Francis Haines's article on the introduction of horses:

> The Nez Perce lined up on one side, each man holding the lead rope of his "trading" horse. Each Spokane came forward and placed his pile of trade goods in front of the horse he liked. If the Nez Perce was satisfied, he handed over the lead rope and took the goods. If not, he might try for an extra article, or he might lead his horse to some other pile which interested him. It might take all of a pleasant summer day to trade 40 horses, but this seemed to worry nobody.

THE ARRIVAL OF THE LEWIS AND CLARK EXPEDITION

In 1805, an event took place that was to have far-reaching consequences for the Nez Perce and other indigenous peoples of the region. In that year, an American expedition led by Meriwether Lewis and William Clark arrived in Nez Perce territory. President Thomas Jefferson authorized the expedition in order to obtain information about the lands and peoples in the newly acquired Louisiana Purchase, territory purchased from the French in 1803.

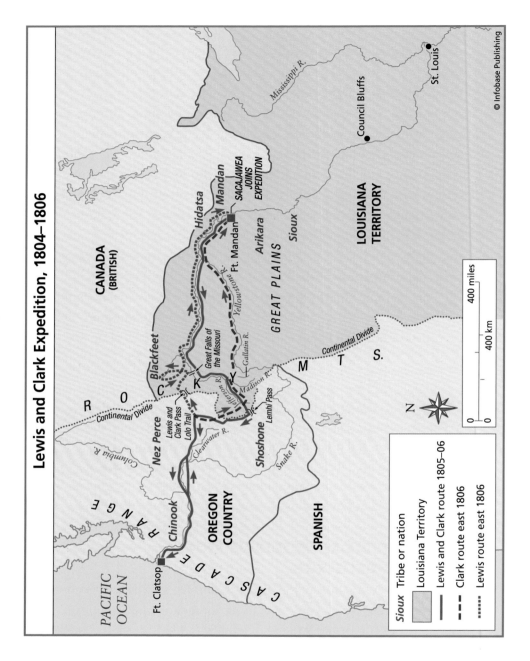

Lewis and Clark Expedition, 1804–1806

© Infobase Publishing

Lewis and Clark's initial passage through Nez Perce lands lasted about one month, from the end of September through the end of October 1805. They then continued westward, and on their return trip they again crossed Nez Perce territory from April through July of 1806. The Lewis and Clark expedition therefore witnessed Nez Perce activity first in the early fall and then from the late spring through midsummer. Their journals, as noted in the previous chapter, provide observations of many features of Nez Perce culture, including their settlements, economic activities, clothing styles, and some aspects of social life. As quoted in a Nez Perce history compiled by Allen Slickpoo and Deward Walker, Clark described his first meeting with members of the Nez Perce village:

> Soon after a man came out to meet me, and with great caution, and conducted me to a large, spacious lodge, which he told me by signs was the lodge of his great chief who had set out three days previous with all the warriors of the nation to war in the southwest direction, and would return in 15 or 18 days. The few men who were left in the village and great numbers of women, gathered around me with much apparent signs of fear, and appeared pleased. They gave us a small piece of buffalo meat, some dried salmon, berries and roots in different states. Of this they make bread and soup. They also gave us the bread made of this root, all of which we ate heartily. I gave them a few small articles as presents, and proceeded on with the chief to his village 2 miles in the same plain, where we were treated kindly in their way, and continued with them all night.

(Opposite page) President Thomas Jefferson sent William Clark and Meriwether Lewis to explore the western United States. Hoping to find the Northwest Passage that would extend straight to the Pacific Ocean, Lewis, Clark, and their crew managed to travel to the California coast but needed help along the way. The Nez Perce, along with other nations, helped protect, teach, and work with the Lewis and Clark expedition.

From the Journals of William Clark

The following excerpt is from the journals of William Clark included in a Nez Perce tribal history edited by Allen Slickpoo and Deward Walker. The entry is dated September 20, 1805. (Spellings and grammar are reprinted here as in the original.)

I Set out early and proceeded on through a Countrey as ruged as usial. Passed over a low mountain into the forks of a large Creek which I kept down 2 miles and assended a Steep mountain leaveing the Creek to our left hand, passed the head of Several dreans on a divideing ridge. And at 12 miles decended the mountain to a leavel pine Countrey. Proceeded on through a butifull Countrey for three miles to a Small Plain in which I found maney Indian lodges, at the distance of 1 mile from the lodges, I met 3 boys, when they Saw me ran and hid themselves in the grass, I dismounted gave my gun and horse to one of the men, searched in the grass and found two of the boys, gave them Small pieces of ribin and Sent them forward to the village. A man Came

Population surveys taken by Lewis and Clark estimated the Nez Perce population to be about 6,000. They were said to be the largest of all of the indigenous groups in the Plateau region. They impressed the Americans, not only with their numbers, but also with their wealth in horses, their expertise as traders, and their hospitality and generosity as hosts. Despite the friendliness of these first encounters, whether unwitting or deliberate, the Lewis and Clark expedition opened the door to disruptions in the lives and security of the Nez Perce and other peoples in the region.

out to meet me with great Caution and Conducted us to a large Spacious Lodge which he told me by Signs was the Lodge of his great Chief who had Set out 3 days previous with all the Warriers of the nation to war on a South West derection and would return in 15 or 18 days. The fiew men that were left in the Village aged, great numbers of women geathered around me with much apparent Signs of fear, and appeared pleased they gave us a Small piece of Buffalow meat. Some dried Salmon beries and roots in different States. Some round and much like an onion which they call quamash the Bread or Take is Sweet. They also gave us the bread made of this root all of which we ate hartily. I gave them a fiew Small articles as preasents, and proceeded on with a Chief to his Village 2 miles in the Same Plain, where we were treated kindly in their way and continued with them all night. Those two Villages consist of about 30 double lodges, but fiew men a number of women and children. They call themselves Cho-pun-nish or Pierced Noses. Their dress has beads white and blue principally, brass and Cop her in different forms. Shells and ware their hare. They are large Portley men Small women and handsom fetured.

EUROPEAN AND AMERICAN TRADERS ENTER THE REGION

In the early nineteenth century, following in the footsteps of Lewis and Clark, American and European traders established commercial relations with Native Americans in the Plateau. Their initial interest was in acquiring animal furs, especially beaver, extending the reach of the fur trade that had begun in the east of North America in the sixteenth century and somewhat later on the Pacific Coast. Even before the nineteenth century, European traders along the Pacific Coast had intruded themselves into the indigenous

Columbia River trading system by supplying new articles, especially metal tools and utensils, shell and glass beads, and later guns and ammunition, that were then traded and re-traded along the indigenous networks.

British fur companies, such as the North West Company and the Hudson's Bay Company, initially established trading posts near the centers of indigenous trade that had been operating for centuries along the Columbia River and its tributaries. One of these was opened in Nez Perce territory by the North West Company in 1812. Named Fort Nez Perce (later called Fort Walla Walla), it was situated at the joining of the Snake and Clearwater rivers. The Nez Perce were glad to trade at this post because of its convenience. They mostly traded horses and beaver furs, and they received a wide variety of articles such as metal tools and utensils, blankets, shell and glass beads, and ornaments. However, from the point of view of the company, the amount of trade brought in by the Nez Perce was disappointing. According to one of the company's agents, writing in 1829 and quoted in Slickpoo and Walker's tribal history:

> The Post has never been very productive, as the country in its neighborhood is not rich [in beaver], and the Natives who are a bold warlike race do little else than rove about in search of scalps, plunder and amusement. It is necessary, however, on many accounts, to keep on good terms with them, and to maintain the post for their accommodation whether it pays or not.

These words exaggerate the "warlike" nature of the Nez Perce but do acknowledge their regional prominence. It was also true, as noted, that the supply of beaver in Nez Perce territory was relatively scarce and quickly depleted because of overhunting.

The Nez Perce then maneuvered to set themselves up as middlemen in trade between the Hudson's Bay Company (which had bought out the North West Company) and Native American

In response to the growing European demand for beaver skins, trading posts were established in the Pacific Northwest. Trading businesses like the Hudson's Bay Company and the North West Company frequently made transactions with Native Americans, including the Nez Perce, allowing them to exchange their furs for firearms, ammunition, and other items.

groups living far from the posts. This strategy proved successful for several decades, but eventually the company sent its men into the interior to trade directly with indigenous peoples. American companies, heading northwest from St. Louis, competed with the British Hudson's Bay Company, establishing posts and sending trappers into the Plateau region. The first post among the Nez Perce was opened in 1829 by traders from the Rocky Mountain Fur Company. By the 1840s, trapping and trading with interior peoples essentially eliminated the middleman role that the Nez Perce had adopted.

At first, Native Americans insisted on embedding commercial transactions within the kind of social relationships that characterized their own trading networks. The British complied with this etiquette, holding feasts and ceremonial gift exchanges with indigenous peoples. American merchants were less likely to adhere to these norms, instead focusing solely on trade as an economic matter divorced from social relations. For their part, indigenous peoples, and particularly the Nez Perce, tried to get the better bargain by encouraging competition between the British and American traders, attempting to lower the prices for the goods they wanted to receive. This strategy was successful for several decades, but by the middle of the nineteenth century most of the companies had departed the region because of the depletion of beaver in the area.

Deepening involvement in trade led to several changes in Nez Perce cultural practices. Prior to the arrival of European and American traders, the Nez Perce economy was balanced and stable. Men and women obtained resources in their territory but were careful not to extract more plants or kill more animals than was necessary, so that these resources could reproduce and be sustained for countless generations. After the people became involved in trade, they began to spend more time obtaining the products that the European and American merchants wanted, principally horses and buffalo hides and meat. In order to acquire the buffalo hides, Nez Perce men had to make more frequent and prolonged journeys eastward into the plains of Montana where the buffalo were numerous. In doing so, they risked confrontations with indigenous peoples in that region, particularly the Flathead. Raiding and intertribal warfare then increased, resulting in casualties on all sides. The Nez Perce obtained horses both through trade with and raiding against other indigenous peoples.

Secondly, American and European traders encouraged Nez Perce men to take more than one wife, a type of marriage called *polygyny*. In traditional Nez Perce society, it was possible for a man to be married to more than one woman, but the practice was not common. The increase in polygyny was associated with demands of the market in buffalo hides. In order for buffalo hides to be marketable, they had to be prepared through a process called tanning, which involved softening the hide. This took many days to accomplish. Since it was the women who prepared the hides, a man with only one wife could supply few hides for trade whereas a man with several wives could increase his participation in trade and therefore increase his wealth and social status.

Trade had an additional negative side as well. By the early nineteenth century, some groups were receiving guns and ammunition from European and American sources. Some guns were obtained directly from the Euro-American traders, while others were obtained from indigenous people through a series of exchanges. Members of villages living along the Columbia River closest to the commercial centers tried to monopolize the trade in weapons in order to prevent peoples living upriver, including the Nez Perce, from obtaining them. But the upriver people sought to open up the trade. Once the Nez Perce had successfully acquired guns through other sources, they attacked several of the Columbia River villages in 1811 and 1814. Raids and retaliations continued to occur throughout the first half of the nineteenth century as different groups vied with each other for access to trade and for dominance in the region. The Nez Perce were generally successful in this competition because of their supply of guns and horses.

SETTLERS AND MISSIONARIES

In addition to introducing the Nez Perce and other indigenous peoples to new goods, the traders opened the way for other groups of Euro-Americans who developed interests in the region. Most notably, these included missionaries who began their attempts to convert indigenous peoples to Christianity in the 1830s, and settlers who began arriving along the Oregon Trail in the 1840s. Between 1845 and 1847, some 10,000 American settlers passed through Plateau territory. The presence of both settlers and missionaries, and the U.S. government that supported them, had far-reaching consequences for the stability and security of the Nez Perce and other Plateau peoples. New forces were at play as the intrusion of American settlers and the extension of American power tipped the balance in their favor.

By the 1830s, both Roman Catholic and Presbyterian missionaries were visiting Nez Perce villages and establishing missions among them. The Presbyterians proved to be the most successful. However, although some Nez Perce seemed interested in having the missionaries work in their communities, there were few early converts. Some of these early converts were village and band headmen who hoped to benefit from their association with the American missionaries, gaining greater access to trade goods and influence. They further hoped to become middlemen in trade between the outsiders and their own village members, supplying people with desired articles and therefore gaining supporters and allies.

A reason for the lack of enthusiasm for conversion on the part of most Nez Perce was that, according to their own traditions, ritual practice was understood to lead to the maintenance of good health, prosperity, and power. But since people who converted to Christianity did not seem to be more likely than others to have these advantages, there was no perceived benefit to following the Christian path. In addition, the rivalries and struggles for power that ensued among headmen who had converted were sometimes disruptive to village and community stability. Nez Perce religious practices remained strong, continuing to furnish the people with a coherent understanding of the world in which they lived.

Despite all of their longings for stability, new challenges would force the Nez Perce to change or abandon some of their traditions under increasing pressure from American settlers and government authorities.

Facing Many Challenges

In the second half of the nineteenth century, the Nez Perce faced many challenges to their community life. These challenges affected their economies, social systems, leadership structure, and religious practices. In addition, their numbers declined drastically as a result of the spread of epidemic diseases in their villages. The most fundamental challenges that they faced were the loss of millions of acres of their lands and the loss of their freedom and independence.

THE SPREAD OF DISEASE

One of the deadliest effects of contact between indigenous peoples and Europeans was the spread of infectious diseases. Native Americans had no natural immunities or resistances to these illnesses, because these diseases had never before been present on the North American continent. These diseases, especially smallpox, measles, influenza, dysentery, and whooping cough, decimated indigenous populations throughout the hemisphere. The depopulation began as early as the sixteenth century in some places and continued well into the nineteenth century in other communities.

Just as different plants and animals originate in specific regions of the world, the organisms that cause disease arise in certain places. Prior to the arrival of Europeans in North America, the bacteria and viruses that cause smallpox, measles, and influenza were unknown on the continent. When these organisms were introduced to populations who had no previous exposure to them, they had devastating effects. People with no natural immunities succumbed in great number. People of all ages were affected, leading to a general decline in population. The deadly organisms were spread either from direct contact with Europeans or from contact with other indigenous people who had contact with the foreigners. Indeed, the earliest epidemics to reach the Plateau were brought through the same intertribal networks that the Nez Perce and others used to obtain trade goods.

Although population estimates before European contact and recordkeeping are always questionable, the Plateau region as a whole was probably inhabited by at least 87,000 people in earlier times. Even this number is likely to be an underestimate of the actual population because it is based on figures collected by missionaries, travelers, and government agents well after the first waves of disease spread through the region.

The earliest documented smallpox epidemic in the Plateau occurred sometime in the 1770s. It originated in communities along the Pacific Coast, where Europeans first arrived in 1774. According to Robert Boyd in his article on smallpox epidemics, observers at the time noted that this epidemic was "a dreadful visitation" with the "most virulent form of the smallpox." Among the Nez Perce, "the people almost to an individual dead. Only here [and] there one survived the disease." Modern population researchers estimate that at least 40 percent of the Native American population in the Plateau region died during this first epidemic.

A second deadly wave of smallpox hit the Plateau in 1801 and 1802. This episode may have originated in the Plains, brought to the Plateau by Nez Perce and other hunters seeking the buffalo that lived in that region. Although many people died during this period, the disease seems to have been in a milder form, causing fewer casualties. Smallpox entered the region in epidemic form two more times, in 1853 and in 1862, causing additional deaths.

After trading posts were opened in the Plateau by British and American merchants in the 1820s and 1830s, additional infectious diseases spread through the Native American villages that congregated around the posts, especially in winter when their own food supplies had dwindled. The Nez Perce were especially affected by whooping cough and influenza. Another source of disease came from the offspring of missionaries and settlers, American children who entered the Plateau in the 1830s and 1840s. They brought with them typical childhood diseases such as chickenpox, whooping cough, and measles.

For the Nez Perce, all of these episodes of disease took a heavy toll. While the indigenous population figures are not known, the Lewis and Clark expedition estimated some 6,000 Nez Perce in 1805. By 1865, a government census reported 2,830 tribal members. Their numbers declined to 2,085 in 1890. A further decline to 1,387 was reported by government figures collected in 1927. After that, the Nez Perce population began a slow recovery.

MISSIONARIES AMONG THE NEZ PERCE

Missionaries, teachers, and government agents were the major pushes behind change in Nez Perce culture. The missionaries, who had begun work in Nez Perce villages in the 1840s with few

Arriving at Lapwai Creek, Idaho, in 1836 with his wife Eliza, Henry Spalding established a home and a Christian mission in Nez Perce territory. He developed a relationship with the Nez Perce and provided them with the knowledge and resources on agriculture and the area soon featured orchards and cultivated farms.

supporters, gradually gained an influential following. The most successful of the Christian missions was established at Lapwai Creek, Idaho, in 1836. It was later renamed in honor of its founder, a Presbyterian minister called Henry Spalding.

Some people gravitated toward the missionaries in order to seek alliances with these powerful representatives of American society. Others thought that they would benefit by learning about American customs and beliefs, since they realized the effectiveness of American power. Some were undoubtedly attracted by the ritual practice in Christian churches. However, tensions eventually surfaced between the missionaries and those Nez Perce who resisted conversion. Tensions also arose between Nez Perce followers of Christianity and those who adhered to traditional beliefs.

The missionaries' attitude toward Nez Perce customs was ambivalent. They admired certain aspects of Nez Perce society, particularly the people's generosity and hospitality, not only toward their own relatives and community members but toward strangers as well. However, the missionaries objected to and therefore tried to convince people to alter or eliminate customs that they thought violated Christian principles or were incompatible with a Euro-American way of life. These included rituals that involved drumming, dancing, and singing and vision quests seeking tutelary spirits. They also opposed the freedom with which Nez Perce men and women engaged in sexual activity prior to marriage and the ease with which they might seek to end an unhappy marriage. Instead, the missionaries encouraged practices consistent with Christian and American ideals: Marriage to only one partner at a time (called monogamy), stable marriages without divorce, keeping of the Sabbath, and attendance at Christian rituals.

Missionaries also promoted changes in Nez Perce economic and social life. They urged people to abandon their foraging strategies and instead become farmers. They encouraged men to become the farmers while women were taught to do household tasks such as cooking and cleaning. This new pattern of work fundamentally affected the roles of men and women. In the past, both women and men contributed directly to the foods that sustained their families. Indeed, women's work contributed more than half of their household nutrition. But with the change in roles advocated by the missionaries, men were to do the major work of providing for their families whereas women's occupations became secondary and supportive. This new pattern was in keeping with American norms but contradicted Nez Perce traditions.

A further change promoted by the missionaries altered the household arrangements of Nez Perce society. In the past, Nez Perce households were based on an extended family structure. An elder couple typically headed a household that included their children and their married children's families. The new pattern emphasized nuclear household arrangements consisting of a married couple and their children. The husband (and father) was considered the head of these new households. This arrangement copied the Euro-American tradition but again violated Nez Perce customs. In Nez Perce traditions, elder men and women jointly exerted influence and authority in relation to other household members. Just as the change in economic roles diminished the importance of women, the change in household arrangements also favored men's positions and made women secondary members. In James's collection of women's voices, contemporary Nez Perce women recall the words of their mothers and grandmothers commenting on these changes:

> Women were involved side-by-side with men in all walks of their lives. In the Nez Perce culture, indirect involvement of women or their presence with men was sufficient to influence political discussions . . . Women did have leadership and power and they were kind of looked to as counselors. These women were from chieftain families as well as from the common families. It was quite an accomplishment; they could be someone.

In addition, missionaries introduced new punishments to be handed out both to adults and children who violated specific rules and regulations drawn up by the ministers. From the Nez Perce point of view, these punishments, which included whippings and hangings, seemed especially harsh. A Nez Perce tribal history recalls Reverend Spalding's list of offenses and punishments, which included the following:

- Whoever willfully takes a life shall be hung.
- Whoever burns a dwelling house shall be hung.
- Whoever burns an outbuilding shall be imprisoned six months, receive fifty lashes, and pay all damages.
- If any one steal, he shall pay back two fold, and if it be the value of a beaver skin or less, he shall receive twenty-five lashes and if the value is over a beaver skin, . . . he shall receive fifty lashes.
- If anyone enter a field and injure the crops, or throw down the fence so that cattle and horses shall go in and do damage, he shall pay all damages and receive twenty-five lashes for every offence.

Although missionaries in the nineteenth century may not have convinced a large number of Nez Perce to convert, they did lead the way for other intruders into Nez Perce territory. Settlers, protected by the American military, soon entered indigenous lands. Government agents followed, establishing posts from which they sought to control the indigenous peoples. These developments were summed up by a Nez Perce observer in Slickpoo and Walker's tribal history:

> The introduction of missionaries . . . played an important role in breaking down our way of life, demoralizing and weakening our cultural values, and ending our power and freedom so that we would be dependent on the whites.
>
> To do this the missionaries came and taught new ways which were alien to us. The military followed to enforce these teachings and clear the way to the vast numbers of encroaching settlers, miners and traders. We asked for the Bible, and that's all we have left.

TREATIES AND RESERVATIONS

In addition to traders and missionaries, government officials extended their reach into the Northwest in order to obtain Native American lands for settlement. They also went to "pacify" the indigenous tribes inhabiting the region so that settlers could enter the territory without fear of attack. In addition, the government sought to establish reservations for Native Americans, to convince them to remain there, and to alter many of their cultural traditions.

The first step in this process was the creation of Oregon Territory in 1848 by an act of the U.S. Congress. The act protected the "rights of person or property" of Native American inhabitants "so long as such rights shall remain unextinguished by treaty." Following the wording of this act, the government set out to negotiate treaties with the indigenous peoples in order to obtain their land, impose cultural changes, and control their destinies. Military posts

may. 1855. Walla Walla Council. Governor Stevens with Indians.

As the United States continued to expand westward, there was a growing urgency to claim more land. Regional councils consisting of Native Americans, local missionaries, and government representatives gathered to allocate territory to different groups, often to the detriment of local indigenous groups. When the Council of Walla Walla (*above*) concluded, the Nez Perce only received 50 percent of the land they had originally occupied.

were opened throughout the Plateau in the 1850s to enable the government to keep close supervision of the region. In addition, the federal Bureau of Indian Affairs sent superintendents to oversee local operations. Henry Spalding was appointed superintendent of the entire eastern Plateau regional office.

The governor of the newly created Oregon Territory, Isaac Stevens, began negotiating treaties in 1854. In the following year, he concluded the Walla Walla Treaty with indigenous nations of the southern Plateau, including the Nez Perce. This treaty established three reservations, including one for the Nez Perce that consisted of about 7,787,000 acres (3,151,300 hectares), located in an area situated in western Idaho, eastern Oregon, and a small amount of acreage in southeastern Washington. This represents a reduction of their aboriginal territory of some 13,000,000 acres (5,260,900 ha), a loss of nearly 50 percent of their land. In return for the land loss, the government agreed to make payments to the tribe of $100,000 during the first two years and an additional $200,000 over the next 20 years. These funds were to be spent on establishing and maintaining schools, health services, and agricultural services. According to the Nez Perce tribal history, Governor Stevens outlined the government's wishes at the treaty council:

> My children, we want you to agree to live on tracts of land, which shall be your own and your children's; we want you to sell the land you do not need to your Great Father; we want you to agree with us upon the payments for these lands; we want you to have schools and mills and shops and farms; we want your people to learn to read and write; your men and boys to be farmers or millwrights or mechanics, or to be of some profession as a lawyer or doctor. We want your wives and daughters to learn to spin and to weave and to make clothes and all the labor of the house.

The words used by Governor Stevens reveal the government's underlying attitude towards the Nez Perce, and indeed, towards all indigenous peoples. The Native Americans were "children" while the government and in particular the president of the United States was the "Great Father." These words also outlined the fundamental goals of culture change: the adoption of farming as the basic economy, changes in the roles of men and women, and residence in permanent communities.

The 1855 treaty guaranteed to the Nez Perce their rights to continue gathering plants, fishing, and hunting on lands ceded to the government as long as the land remained unoccupied by American settlers. It also guaranteed that the government would continue to support schools and agricultural services indefinitely unless limited by further treaties.

Although Nez Perce delegates voiced some opposition to the treaty provisions at the council, eventually their leaders were persuaded to sign it. Governor Stevens stressed the fact that many white settlers were already encroaching on Nez Perce territory, taking their resources and occasionally attacking individuals. Stevens said that the government would only protect the people from further harm if they agreed to the treaty.

Treaties between the Nez Perce and the United States

The following are excerpts from the Treaty of 1855 between leaders of the Nez Perce and the U.S. government that were included in Slickpoo and Walker's Nez Perce tribal history:

Article 1. The Nez Perce tribe hereby cede, relinquish, and convey to the United States all their rights, title, and interest in and to the country occupied or claimed by them, bounded and described as follows [The treaty then included a description of the boundaries of the lands ceded to the United States].

Article 2. There is, however, reserved from the lands above ceded for the use and occupation of the said tribe, the tract of land included within the following boundaries [The treaty then provides a description of the boundaries of the lands reserved for the Nez Perce].

All which tract shall be set apart for the exclusive use and benefit of said tribe as an Indian reservation; nor shall any white man, except those in the employment of the Indian Department, be permitted to reside upon the said reservation without the permission of the tribe and the superintendent and the agent.

Article 3. The exclusive right of taking fish in all streams where running through or bordering said reservation is further secured to said Indians; as also the right of taking fish at all usual and accustomed places in common with citizens of the Territory; together with the privilege of hunting, gathering roots and berries,

In 1863, only eight years after the government guaranteed the Nez Perce ownership of their reservation, a second treaty was negotiated. A new treaty council was called shortly after gold was discovered in lands on and near the Nez Perce Indian Reservation,

and pasturing their horses and cattle upon open and unclaimed land.

Article 4. In consideration of the above cession, the United States agreed to pay to the said tribe the sum of $200,000. All which said sums of money shall be applied to the use and benefit of the said Indians.

Article 5. The United States further agrees to establish within said reservation two schools, provided with furniture and books, one of which shall be an agricultural and industrial school, and to employ two teachers; to build two blacksmiths' shops, a tin shop, and a gunsmith's shop; one carpenter's shop, one wagon and plough-maker's shop, and to furnish with the necessary tools; to erect one sawmill and one flour mill; to erect a hospital, provided with the necessary medicines and furniture, and to employ a physician.

Below are excerpts from another treaty, this one signed in 1863 between a number of Nez Perce leaders and the U.S. government.

Article 1. The said Nez Perce tribe agree to relinquish, and do hereby relinquish, to the United States the lands heretofore reserved for the use and occupation of the said tribe, saving and accepting so much thereof as is described in Article 2 for a new reservation.

Article 2. The United States agree to reserve for a home, and for the sole use and occupation of the said tribe, the tract of land included within the following boundaries. [The treaty then provides a description of the new boundaries for the reduced Nez Perce Reservation.]

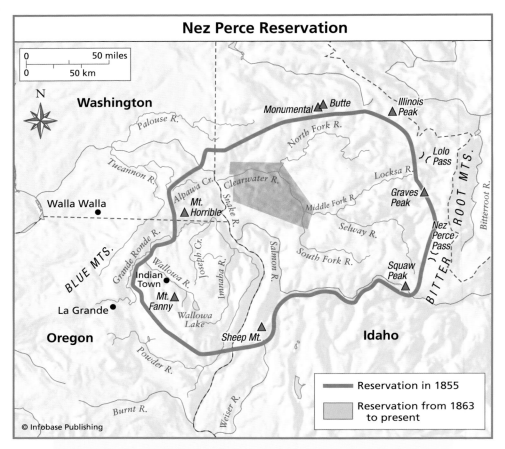

During the Council of Walla Walla in 1855, the Nez Perce protested the loss of their lands, but government authorities assured them that this was a beneficial development. Nearly a decade later in 1963, gold miners and settlers flooded the area and another council determined that more Nez Perce land would be allotted to these newcomers.

attracting an enormous influx of nearly 10,000 settlers and prospectors by 1861. The major provision of the treaty made a further reduction in Nez Perce territory, taking away the lands that contained the gold reserves as well as additional acreage. Of the original 7,787,000-acre (3,151,300-ha) reservation, only 757,000 acres (306,347 ha) remained, a loss of more than 7,000,000 acres (2,832,800 ha) or about 90 percent of their land.

This treaty was, and still is, controversial because the Nez Perce negotiators who were invited to the treaty negotiations and who signed the document were members of the so-called Upper Nez Perce and did not actually represent the entire tribe. In fact, the chiefs who signed were heads of bands that lived on lands included in the reduced reservation, while leaders of bands whose lands were signed away were not present at the treaty council. The government agents favored the Upper Nez Perce because they were thought to be more likely to agree to government wishes. The majority of the Upper Nez Perce were Christians and were more receptive to policies that encouraged cultural change than were the so-called Lower Nez Perce, the majority of whom followed the traditional religion and were more resistant to government policies. The Lower Nez Perce objected to the new treaty, and especially to giving away more of their lands.

After the treaty was enforced, antagonisms between the two groups of Nez Perce grew into open conflicts. At the same time, a new wave of Presbyterian missionary activity began in Nez Perce communities. Members of the Upper Nez Perce converted in large numbers while very few members of the Lower Nez Perce did so. Instead, they retained faith in their indigenous forms of belief and practice. This contrast in religion served to heighten the growing rift between the two communities.

A final treaty was signed in 1868 that clarified some of the provisions of the Treaty of 1863. In particular, it guaranteed to the Nez Perce their rights to the resources on their lands, especially to the timber reserves that American companies were trying to access.

The provisions of these treaties, with the loss of land and livelihood, led quickly to disagreement among the Nez Perce. The division between the Upper Nez Perce, living near the administrative center at Lapwai, and the Lower Nez Perce, living in an area about 100 miles (160 kilometers) south, created conflicts over land and cultural changes that have continued into the twenty-first century. The treaties also immediately led to attempts by some Nez Perce to escape from the control exerted by the U.S. government in the 1870s. Some people resisted through military means while others forged new cultural practices that expressed their Nez Perce identities.

Fighting to be Free

In the latter half of the nineteenth century, the Nez Perce confronted a situation filled with many challenges. They had lost the major portion of their traditional homelands. They could no longer gather plants in all of the environments that they had been accustomed to. They could no longer fish and hunt in their ancient territories. The people were forced into a new way of living, with new rules and regulations not of their choosing. They sent their children to schools to learn a foreign language and to learn foreign customs, values, and beliefs.

Some of the people accepted these changes and set about to conform to the policies and preferences of the schoolteachers, missionaries, and U.S. government agents. They hoped that with these actions they would find peace, security, and prosperity. Others among the Nez Perce resisted these changes, desiring instead to maintain their traditional customs, to continue to practice their own religions, and to speak their own language. In any society, resistance can take many forms. It can take the overt form of direct confrontation, or it can take the covert form of rejecting foreign customs and maintaining or reworking one's own practices.

WARFARE AND RESISTANCE

By the 1870s, most of the Nez Perce were living on the reservation assigned to them in the treaties of 1855 and 1863. Because they had lost the vast majority of their ancestral lands, they could not continue their traditional economic practices of gathering, fishing, and hunting to the degree that they had done before. Foragers need to have access to large territories because they need to be able to use plant and animal resources that are seasonally available in different areas. Therefore, many of the Nez Perce adapted themselves to farming in keeping with the plans advocated by government agents. They planted wheat, various vegetables and fruit crops. Women gathered the wild roots and fruits available nearby. Most men continued to fish in local rivers and streams. In addition, some men journeyed eastward into the plains of Montana in order to hunt buffalo, taking the meat and hides for their own uses as well as for trade with other indigenous peoples and with the Americans.

There were, however, some Nez Perce who refused to adopt the lifestyle imposed upon them by the U.S. government. Prominent among these were the people who lived in the band headed by a man whose Native American name was Hin-mah-too-yah-lat-kekht, meaning "thunder rolling in the mountains." He came to be known in English as Chief Joseph. This band lived in the Wallowa Valley of northeastern Oregon. When the Treaty of 1855 was agreed, land in the Wallowa Valley was included as part of the Nez Perce Indian Reservation; but when the Treaty of 1863 was drawn up, these lands were ceded to the United States. Chief Joseph and his followers were not signatories to that treaty and therefore refused to accept their loss of land.

In 1873, in response to their objections, U.S. president Ulysses S. Grant agreed to a plan offered by the Bureau of Indian Affairs and created the separate Wallowa Reservation for Chief Joseph's band. Conflict over this land continued, however, because American settlers pressured the government to reverse its decision so that they

Chief Joseph, one of the most famous members of the Nez Perce, strongly opposed handing over his tribe's ancestral lands to the incoming settlers and prospectors and refused to conform to life on the reservation. Honoring the traditions of his father, Joseph tried to preserve his people's territory and their way of life.

could have access to the excellent grazing and farming lands there. Armed clashes between Nez Perce living at Wallowa and intruding settlers occurred from time to time, creating bitterness between the two groups. In 1875, President Grant abandoned his promise to the Nez Perce of Wallowa and declared that their lands were no longer a reservation, instead opening the area for American settlement.

A U.S. Army general, Oliver Howard, was assigned the task of either convincing or forcing Chief Joseph and his followers to leave Wallowa and take up residence on the Nez Perce Indian Reservation in Idaho. A series of meetings began in May 1877 between Nez Perce leaders and the U.S. Army. The difference in attitudes held by the Nez Perce and U.S. negotiators can be summed up by two statements, one from Nez Perce Chief Toohulhulsote and one from General Howard, as quoted in Alvin Josephy's *The Nez Perce Indians and the Opening of the Northwest*:

> *Chief Toohulhulsote:* "You white people measure the Earth and divide it. The Earth is part of my body, and I never gave up the Earth. I belong to the land out of which I came. The Earth is my mother."
>
> *General Howard:* "We do not wish to interfere with your religion, but you must talk about practical things. Twenty times over you have repeated the Earth is your mother, and that chieftainship is from the Earth. Let us hear it no more, but come to business at once . . ."

The Nez Perce finally agreed to relocate to the reservation. They were given 30 days to make the move. Even though the people felt that this was not enough time, they packed their belongings and began to move toward the reservation in Idaho. As they were

(Opposite page) In spite of his efforts to preserve the peace among his people and the U.S. army, Chief Joseph and his followers were soon fighting and fleeing at the same time. Although they were outnumbered, this small contingent of the Nez Perce managed to hold off U.S. military forces and almost made it over the border and into Canada.

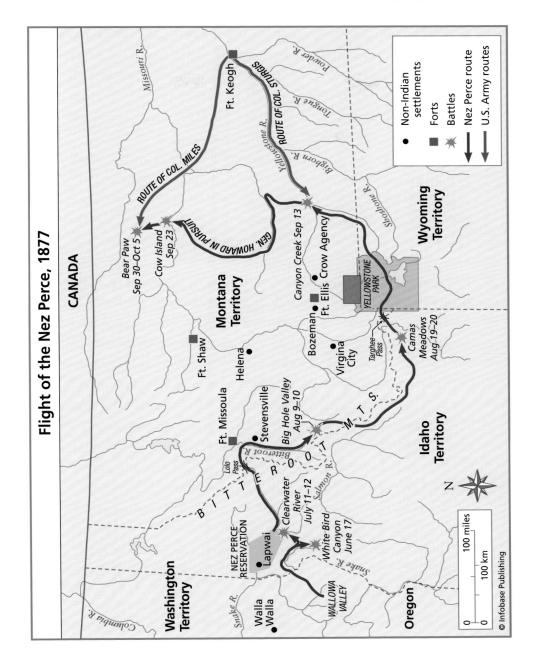

Flight of the Nez Perce, 1877

CANADA

Washington
Territory

Montana
Territory

Idaho
Territory

Wyoming
Territory

Oregon

Missouri R.

Powder R.

Tongue R.

Yellowstone R.

Bighorn R.

Shoshone R.

Ft. Keogh

ROUTE OF COL. MILES

ROUTE OF COL. STURGIS

GEN. HOWARD IN PURSUIT

Bear Paw
Sep 30–Oct 5

Cow Island
Sep 23

Canyon Creek Sep 13

Ft. Ellis

Crow Agency

Bozeman

Virginia
City

Ft. Shaw

Helena

Ft. Missoula

Stevensville

Big Hole Valley
Aug 9–10

Lolo
Pass

B I T T E R R O O T   M T S.

Bitterroot R.

Clearwater
River
July 11–12

Salmon R.

White Bird
Canyon
June 17

Snake R.

NEZ PERCE
RESERVATION

Lapwai

WALLOWA
VALLEY

Walla
Walla

Snake R.

Columbia R.

YELLOWSTONE
PARK

Targhee
Pass

Camas
Meadows
Aug 19–20

N

● Non-Indian
  settlements

■ Forts

✴ Battles

↓ Nez Perce route

↓ U.S. Army routes

0   100 miles
0   100 km

© Infobase Publishing

traveling, confusion reigned about the military's intentions and feelings of anger and betrayal arose on the part of many of the Nez Perce. Some young men in the Nez Perce village of Whitehead, angered by previous killings of Native Americans by American settlers, decided to seek revenge. The settlers retaliated by waging more attacks against Nez Perce communities.

In that atmosphere, General Howard decided to assert control and arrest people at Whitehead. When soldiers under the command of Captain David Perry, one of General Howard's captains, arrived at the village, a battle ensued that ended in a Nez Perce victory even though they were outnumbered and poorly armed. General Howard then sent a larger contingent out against the Nez Perce, who at that point decided to seek safety away from the reservation. Several important battles occurred as the soldiers followed Chief Joseph and the men and women of his band, who numbered somewhere between 700 and 750. In these battles, the Nez Perce emerged victorious. They were able to escape capture during a period of three months, first moving east toward the plains, through Yellowstone National Park, and then turning north through Montana, hoping to find refuge in Canada.

Thinking that General Howard and his army were farther behind than they actually were, Chief Joseph and his people stopped to set up a camp and gather supplies for their last trek into Canada. General Howard was in fact close behind, and surprised them at Bear Paws in Montana, just 40 miles (65 km) from the Canadian border. According to the Nez Perce tribal history, after a long battle, Chief Joseph surrendered, handing his rifle to General Howard and stating:

> I am tired of fighting. Our chiefs are killed. The old men are all dead. It is the young men who say yes or no. He who led the young men is dead. It is cold and we have no blankets. The little children are freezing to death. My people, some of them, have run away to the hills and have no blankets, no food; no one knows where they are, perhaps freezing to death. I want to

have time to look for my children and see how many of them I can find. Maybe I shall find them among the dead. Hear me, my chiefs, I am tired; my heart is sick and sad. From where the sun now stands, I will fight no more, forever.

The series of battles was finally drawn to a close. Some 120 Nez Perce (65 men and 55 women and children) had been killed by the army, while 177 American soldiers were killed and some 147 others wounded.

Although the earlier goal of the government had been to force Chief Joseph and his followers to move to the Nez Perce Indian Reservation in Idaho, after his surrender they refused to let him join the people who were already residing on the Nez Perce Reservation. Instead, he and the rest of his band, then numbering 431, were ordered to go to Oklahoma and live on lands that were originally part of the Ponca Reservation. Federal agents had first insisted that the band leave the Wallowa Valley to go to the Nez Perce Indian Reservation in Idaho, but after the war ended they refused to let the people return to Idaho. In 1878, ignoring the people's objections, soldiers took the surviving Nez Perce to Fort Leavenworth in Kansas, where they were then taken by train and wagon to Oklahoma. They finally arrived in July, but by October, 47 of the exiles had died, most from exposure to the heat, lack of clean water to drink, and poor sanitation conditions.

For several years, the people tried to eke out a living on their new lands in Oklahoma but despite their efforts, their living conditions continued to be harsh. The death rate, especially among children, was so high that it alarmed local doctors and officials. Indeed, all of the Nez Perce children born in Oklahoma, numbering about 100, died there within a few years. Conditions gradually improved and the people's crops of corn, wheat, potatoes, and melons were successful. Then, in 1884, a severe drought hit the region, resulting in serious crop damage and losses.

Throughout their exile in Oklahoma, Chief Joseph and the Nez Perce petitioned the government to allow them to return to

The Words of Chief Joseph

After the end of the Nez Perce War, Chief Joseph continued to appeal to government officials to allow him and his followers to join their compatriots on the Nez Perce Indian Reservation in Idaho. His appeals gradually gained support from many influential politicians and civil leaders, but the federal government refused to grant their request. The following is an excerpt from a statement by Chief Joseph that was printed in the *North American Review* in April 1879.

> All men were made by the same Great Spirit Chief. They are all brothers. The earth is the mother of all people, and all people should have the equal rights upon it. You might as well expect the rivers to run backward as that any man who was born a free man should be contented penned up and denied liberty to go where he pleases. If you tie a horse to a stake, do you expect he will grow fat? If you pen an Indian up on a small spot of earth, and compel him to stay there, he will not be contented nor will he grow and prosper. I have asked some of the great white chiefs where they get their authority to say to the Indian that he shall stay in one place, while he sees white men going where they please. They cannot tell me. I only ask of the Government to be treated as all other men are treated. If I cannot go to my own home, let me have a home in some country where my people will not die so fast.
>
> Whenever the white man treats the Indian as they treat each other, then we shall have no more wars. We shall be all alike—brothers of one father and one mother, with one sky above us and one country around us, and one government for all. Then the Great Spirit Chief who rules above will smile on this land, and send rain to wash out the bloody spots made by brothers' hands upon the face of the earth. For this time the Indian race are waiting and praying.

their compatriots in Idaho. Many officials and influential private citizens joined their efforts on humanitarian grounds. Finally, in 1885, the people were allowed to go north, but not as a united group. The Nez Perce who were followers of the Presbyterian Church, about 165 in number, were permitted to repatriate to the Lapwai community on the Nez Perce Indian Reservation in Idaho. The non-Christians, also numbering about 160, were instead sent to join other indigenous peoples living on the Colville Reservation in northern Washington. Chief Joseph and his band traveled to Colville as well. Despite Joseph's objections and some resistance on the part of the Native Americans already living on the Colville Reservation, the Nez Perce were forcibly relocated there in 1886. They established a community called Nespelem and once again tried to make a home for themselves.

They struggled to survive at first, to grow crops in a way that was foreign to them, but eventually they began to prosper. Their farmlands became productive and the cattle and horses that they raised increased in number. But still, the people longed to return to the Wallowa Valley, hoping to regain a small amount of their original land in that region. According to Merrill Beal's book about Chief Joseph, in 1901, Joseph said, "My home is in the Wallowa Valley, and I want to go back there to live. My father and mother are buried there. If the government would only give me a small piece of land for my people in the Wallowa Valley, with a teacher, that is all I would ask." However, by that time, the Wallowa Valley was inhabited by American settlers. Therefore, although some influential officials were sympathetic to the Nez Perce appeals, no action was ever taken to allow them to return. Chief Joseph himself died a few years later, in 1904, at the age of 64.

By the last years of the nineteenth century, the Nez Perce had become a divided people. A few never made the journey north and lived side by side with other Native Americans in Oklahoma, far from their homelands. Some lived in Washington State, sharing the Colville Reservation with other Plateau peoples. The majority resided on the Nez Perce Indian Reservation in Idaho. Wherever they lived, the Nez Perce faced many of the same problems, trying to establish a new way of life that would give them security and prosperity.

THE PROPHET DANCE AND THE SEVEN DRUM RELIGION

Resistance to forced changes may take many forms in societies throughout the world. People sometimes resist external control by strengthening and reinforcing their own systems of belief. This type of resistance may come out as religious movements that promote indigenous culture and seek solutions to current problems through spiritual means. These forms of expression are known as *revitalization movements*. Revitalization movements arise in situations of rapid cultural change that undermines traditional beliefs, erodes economic stability, and limits political independence. Such was the situation for the Nez Perce and other indigenous peoples in the Plateau region in the second half of the nineteenth century.

Several such indigenous religious movements found followers in Nez Perce communities. Although these movements were to some degree innovative, they also emphasized a continuation of indigenous beliefs and practices. One of the earliest of these indigenous practices was the Prophet Dance. The ritual itself was a circular dance, with men and women stepping in a rhythmic pattern while singing and praying. Each dance was organized by a leader who had received inspiration in visionary contacts with spirit beings. These visionary experiences usually occurred when a person was thought to have been nearly dead, or was even thought to have actually died.

The vision came in a kind of reawakening or rebirth. The leader or prophet then announced his or her message of hope and renewal for the whole community. The dance was a means of honoring the vision and of hastening the time of world rejuvenation. During the dance, some of the participants also received visions. Dances might be led by different prophets, some of whom might attract a large following if their prophecies and visions were especially compelling.

Several revitalization movements were created after Native American tribes and nations were forced into reservations. The Prophet Dance, one of the most prominent revitalization movements of the Nez Perce, was the precursor of the Ghost Dance (*above*), a similar group that reached reservations all over the country.

Another religious movement that developed in response to the changes wrought in Nez Perce communities in the nineteenth century was called *Washat,* or the *Seven Drum Religion.* In this tradition, ceremonies were also inspired by a leader who received spiritual messages in visions and dreams. He or she imparted prophecies and sometimes performed miraculous cures, often while in a trance state. The ceremony itself centered on drumming and singing. Seven drummers positioned themselves in a row at the western end of the rectangular house, or longhouse, in which the ritual took place. Another participant held a bell, which he rang in time to the drumming. Each drummer, beginning with the youngest, sang songs in succession. At the same time, the men and women in attendance danced and sang, holding fans made of eagle feathers in their right hands. At intervals of rest between the songs and dances, elders from the community might speak to those present, encouraging them to maintain their cultural traditions and beliefs.

Government agents and missionaries were assigned to the Nez Perce Indian Reservation with the task of asserting control. They tried, but failed, to dampen people's interest in these religious movements. Indeed, as the nineteenth century wore on, ceremonies for the Prophet Dance and the Seven Drum Religion drew increasing numbers of participants. These rituals appealed to people because they conveyed messages that validated Nez Perce customs and offered hope to a people overwhelmed by changes that they could not control.

The message of hope and renewal reverberates in some Nez Perce communities today as well. Indeed, the Seven Drum Religion has a growing number of contemporary followers who employ these rituals to enhance their feelings of solidarity as Nez Perce.

A Century
of Change

It is now just a little more than a century since the end of the Nez Perce War and the repatriation of the exiles from Oklahoma to the Nez Perce Indian Reservation in Idaho. Government policies aimed at cultural transformation have brought about many changes in people's lives. Particularly important changes took place in the education system, the rules for land ownership, and local political systems.

EDUCATION

In order to further the goal of promoting changes in Nez Perce behavior and attitudes, government officials established schools for Nez Perce children. Some of the schools were day schools, while others were boarding schools that housed children for the entire school year. Boarding schools were deemed the most effective at promoting new beliefs and values among indigenous peoples, because this kind of school separated children from their homes and families for long periods of time.

All of the schools exposed children to new ways of thinking and acting. Most of the teachers were either missionaries themselves or were assigned by missionary boards that oversaw Native American education. Since the schools were allied with church organizations, they taught values that went along with Christian teachings and American cultural practices. The teachers stressed the importance of obeying authority, whether that authority was a teacher, a missionary, or a government agent. Children were eventually also made to feel ashamed of their parents, of their traditional customs and beliefs, and even of their own language.

Educational policies were spelled out by Edward Geary, superintendent of the Bureau of Indian Affairs for the Pacific Northwest region. As quoted in Stephen Beckham's article about Nez Perce history, Geary wrote in 1859:

> The children educated at these institutions should be taken entirely from the control of their parents, and boarded under the care of a judicious matron, where habits of cleanliness, punctuality, and order should be carefully cultivated. The education of the schools should not only embrace letters, but the boys should be instructed in agriculture and trades; the girls in the use of the needle and the various branches of domestic economy. These schools should be governed and taught by persons of not only capacity, firmness, and ability, but by those of decidedly religious character.

In the 1870s, under the presidency of Ulysses S. Grant, Native American affairs were handled by church boards rather than non-religious agencies. The Nez Perce Indian Reservation, and especially its education system, was given over to the control of the Presbyterian mission. Henry Spalding, the Presbyterian minister who had worked among the Nez Perce from 1836 to 1847, returned as the superintendent in charge of the agency. Religious instruction was merged with training in farming and various trades such as blacksmithing and mechanics for boys and domestic work for girls.

The transfer of schools to religious authorities heightened conflicts between different groups of Nez Perce. Divisions between Christians and non-Christians became more intense as parents who followed traditional beliefs and practices feared the influence of Christian teachers. The fact that Presbyterians ran the schools also created conflict between the majority of Christian Nez Perce who were Presbyterians and the minority who had converted to Catholicism. Gradually, these three communities (Presbyterians, Catholics, and traditionalists) drifted apart to settle in different areas. The Presbyterians resided in the towns of Lapwai and Kamiah in Idaho, the sites of government posts, agencies, and churches. These towns grew to be the politically dominant areas on the Nez Perce lands.

In the late nineteenth century, education on the reservation was in the hands of Presbyterian Church ministers and lay workers who stressed conformity with American customs, beliefs, and values. The basic philosophy of these educators was summed up in 1878 by James Wilbur, agent to the nearby Yakama Reservation, as quoted in Beckham's article:

> The Bible and the plow (which must never be divorced) have brought them up from the horrible pit, and put a new song into their mouths, and new hopes into their hearts. They are washed and clothed in their right minds. There can be no lasting good accomplished with the children in school, without taking them to a boarding school, where they are taught to talk, read, and write the English language.

Schools on the Nez Perce Indian Reservation embraced this philosophy to the utmost. During most of the late nineteenth century, however, very few children actually attended the schools. Those who did later became proponents of accommodation to government policies that promoted cultural changes, not just in education but in work roles, housing styles, and basic family organization. Along with the shift towards farming, the agents favored constructing separate nuclear family dwellings modeled on those of rural America at the time. The intent was not only related to housing styles, but also to household organization; that is, the underlying goal was to break up the large, extended family residential patterns that kept several generations living together, cooperating in their work, and socializing children. It was an attempt to separate generations that, along with schooling, removed children from the direct influence of their families, particularly of their grandparents who were likely to retain traditional cultural practices and ideals.

Based on the Carlisle Indian School in Pennsylvania, the Indian Training School in Oregon separated Native American youths from their families, reservations, and traditions. These young people, some of whom were Nez Perce, were taught to leave their own cultures behind and to adhere to Christian and American customs.

In 1880, a further step in separating children from their families began with the founding of the Indian Training School, located off the reservation in Forest Grove, Oregon. (It later moved to Chemawa, near Salem, Oregon.) The Indian Training School drew students from many reservations in the Northwest, including the Nez Perce. It was a boarding school that included a summer work program so that students would not return to their home communities until they had completed many years of training.

The school operated under an "outing system," first developed for Native American institutions at the Carlisle Indian School in Pennsylvania. In this system, students worked during the summer on the farms and in the homes of American citizens. Boys worked as farm hands and ranch hands, while girls did domestic labor in the households. The children were not paid for their work. The founder of the Indian Training School, M.C. Wilkinson, a lieutenant in the U.S. Army, commented on his intentions, as quoted in Beckham's article: "The first rule here after cleanliness and obedience is 'No Indian Talk.' Children are to be divided up until all tribal association is broken up and lost. Their entire removal from family and reservation influences are the points of highest hope." Children from the Nez Perce Indian Reservation began attending the Indian Training School in 1884, arriving in an initial group of 34.

All of the schools, whether day or boarding, whether on or off the reservation, followed military-style discipline. Corporal punishment was handed out to children who did not follow the many regulations governing their behavior and speech. Children caught speaking in their native language were punished in order to convince them to switch to speaking only English.

Finally, both day and boarding schools stressed the development of patriotism toward the United States. Celebrations for the Fourth of July lasted four full days and included foot races, horse races, feasting, and parades. Soon, celebrations for other national holidays, including George Washington's birthday, Memorial Day, Thanksgiving, and Christmas were added to the list. Observance

Memories of Schooling

Children sent to boarding schools left with unforgettable memories of loneliness, fear, and longing for their families. The following are excerpts from contemporary interviews with Nez Perce elders about that period, included in Caroline James's collection:

The boys had to wear soldiers' outfits. It was based on a military way of conducting school. They had to salute, march, wear caps, and wear uniforms. They weren't allowed to talk Indian. They had to wear nametags. They had to give up their traditions and culture. If they did practice them, they got beaten on their heads. The boys and the girls had to be there on the parade ground. All Indian schools were patterned the same way.

In boarding schools, you did not learn. You did not have your parents there to give you the examples. All you saw was the regimentation of boarding school, rather than a happy face giving you love and companionship, early

of these holidays promoted allegiance to the United States and to Christian beliefs and principles.

LAND ALLOTMENTS

There were also policies aimed at encouraging indigenous peoples to change their systems of land possession. In 1887, the U.S. Congress passed the Dawes Severalty Act (also known as the General Allotment Act). According to this law, lands on Native American reservations were to be assigned as separate allotments to individuals or families who were properly registered on census rolls drawn up by agents in charge of the reservation. Previously, morning when you went to breakfast, somebody to encourage you to go to school.

We had a movie house on campus, and there were movies on Friday night, or maybe a dance to attend, and if you've lost those privileges, you cannot attend. If you did something wrong, you cannot attend. If your room was not cleaned, you cannot attend. We [girls] had to wear dresses, we could not wear pants. The boys had to have short hair. They could not have long hair.

My dad and my uncle would tell stories about how, if they talked their own language, they would be beaten across the hands with a ruler until it was bloody. They would suffer. They would punish them if they continued to speak their own language and keep their own culture.

My grandmother went to boarding school when she was 13 or 14, and she stayed there until she was a young woman, maybe 20 or so. A lot of what they did was learning domestic help. And there were Indian people from all over, and then she would work during vacations and all through summer. They would assign them to some of the rich families in that area to be their domestic help.

reservation lands were held communally by the tribe as a collective entity.

The new law provided that families would receive 160 acres (65 ha) while individuals living alone would receive 80 acres (32 ha) each. The act further provided that any land remaining after each eligible person had received their allotment would be declared "surplus" and be available for claim by American homesteaders. The law further stipulated that a Native American landowner could sell his or her acreage to an outsider at the end of a period of 25 years after allotment. This policy therefore had a dual effect: It broke up the communal nature of indigenous landholding, and it withdrew millions of acres of reservation land from Native American control. Indeed, nationwide, more than 60 million acres (24,281,000 ha) of indigenous land was lost. By 1934, two-thirds of all land that had been allotted to Native Americans, amounting to some 27 million acres (10,926,500 ha), was also lost.

On the Nez Perce Indian Reservation, a policy called Allotment began in 1890. In the first year, 1,000 allotments were assigned, with an additional 905 allotments made by 1893. Some of the best parcels were immediately taken by white men who had married Nez Perce women. Then, after continued pressure from the U.S. government, in 1893, Nez Perce leaders agreed to sell some additional 542,000 acres (219,340 ha) of "surplus" lands in exchange for about $1,626,000. Of this money, $1 million was channeled into a trust fund for collective use, while the remainder was distributed equally to registered Nez Perce members. Nez Perce allotments amounted to 182,938 acres (74,032 ha), leaving only 32,020 acres (12,958 ha) in tribal trust. The total land base, then, was 214,958 acres (86,990 ha) by the turn of the twentieth century. Soon, however, an additional 130,000 acres (52,610 ha) were sold or otherwise lost by individuals or families.

In all, the Nez Perce homeland of 13 million acres was reduced to fewer than 80,000 acres by the year 1975. It has since increased to about 88,000 acres through the success of tribal policies of acquiring land that had previously been sold or lost. But the legacy of past actions is reflected in the fact that more than 85 percent of the land within the Nez Perce Indian Reservation is owned by people who are not Native Americans. The land that *is* still owned by the Nez Perce is a patchwork of allotments scattered throughout the territory.

THE MERIAM REPORT

In 1926, in response to reports of dire economic and social conditions on many Native American reservations throughout the

United States, Congress authorized a survey to be carried out by the Bureau of Indian Affairs to document and assess living conditions. The survey resulted in a report two years later, called the Meriam Report, after its organizer Lewis Meriam. It recommended that new federal policies be instituted to alleviate some of the worst conditions of poverty, poor education, poor health, and substandard housing that existed on many reservations.

The survey conducted on the Nez Perce Indian Reservation indicated a great deal of variation in living standards. Most of the older residents lived in good homes, had productive gardens, and kept some domesticated animals such as chickens, horses, and cattle. However, younger residents tended to live with their elders without establishing independent households of their own. When they did set up their own households, they tended to be poor and to live in substandard housing. In all cases, the report documented the increasing reliance of Nez Perce members on rental income obtained from leasing their lands to white farmers and ranchers. Indeed, the report investigators counted about 1,300 Nez Perce and about 20,000 white people living on the reservation.

In addition to documenting living conditions on reservations, the Meriam Report outlined a number of positions relating to federal policy regarding Native Americans. The report condemned the General Allotment Act of 1887 and criticized the shrinkage of indigenous territory and the breakup of communal lands into individual parcels. It also criticized the educational system operating on most reservations that forced children to leave their families to be schooled in boarding schools. Finally, the report urged for tribal groups to have more power to make decisions concerning programs and policies affecting their communities, including their right to maintain their language and cultural traditions if they chose to do so.

Leading from the data uncovered by the Meriam Report and the broad outline of policies it recommended, the Nez Perce formed a tribal organization called the Nez Perce Indian Home and

Farm Association. The association consisted of a general council that included all adult members of the tribe. The association also created a business committee charged with proposing and implementing economic development plans for the reservation.

At one of its first meetings, the newly formed Nez Perce Committee drew up its "Declaration of Purpose." Included in this statement, which was reprinted in the Nez Perce tribal history, was a summary of the forces at work that led to the situation in which the Nez Perce found themselves at that time:

> We see many of our people—particularly our young people—without permanent homes of their own, and in many cases, leasing to white men the land which they themselves should farm. We see neglected homes, and children growing up without proper parental guidance and control; we see the majority of our people depending on the income from their leased lands for their support; we see our allotted land and the homes of our fathers gradually passing into the hands of the white man—title to more than 900, or almost one half of the original allotments having thus passed, leaving many of our people without land.

The association drew up a five-year plan aimed at improving homes and living conditions and encouraging people to farm their own lands rather than leasing them to outsiders. In addition, its basic goal was to get people involved in their own communities. To this end, 15 local chapters were established throughout the reservation so that people could more easily participate in tribal affairs.

ESTABLISHING TRIBAL GOVERNANCE

As an outgrowth of community organizing in conjunction with the Nez Perce Indian Home and Farm Association, meetings of all adult members of the tribe formulated a "body of consent" for the development of a governing constitution. A tribal committee drafted a constitution that was finally approved in 1927 by officials in the Bureau of Indian Affairs.

According to its provisions, the governing body of the reservation, known as the Advisory Council and Business Committee of the Nez Perce Reservation, had nine members, all elected by the adult members of the Nez Perce tribe. The committee met four times each year to discuss tribal affairs. The group's functions included approving land leases, loan applications, timber sales permits, and grazing permits. In addition, the committee pursued land claims suits against the federal government. However, although the committee considered a wide range of issues, no actions could be taken without the consent of the Bureau of Indian Affairs in keeping with federal policy regarding Native Americans. The committee therefore was not truly an independent body and lacked the authority that would have made it a sovereign body. Lacking real independence, the Nez Perce Committee could not put new policies into action nor could it disburse funds for programs in the communities.

THE INDIAN REORGANIZATION ACT

A new direction in federal policy on Native Americans was ushered in during the 1930s under the leadership of the Commissioner of Indian Affairs, John Collier. As commissioner, Collier put into practice a number of guiding principles, including recognizing the uniqueness of indigenous cultures and supporting the maintenance of Native languages and of traditional cultural and religious practices. In response to Collier's advocacy, Congress passed the Wheeler-Howard Bill in 1934, also known as the Indian Reorganization Act or IRA.

The IRA had several major provisions that altogether enhanced the ability of tribes to begin the process of self-governance. Funds were earmarked to establish agricultural and industrial credit systems for use by tribal governments. Funds were also set aside for training programs in administration and various professions. In

The Indian Reorganization Act (IRA), also know as the Wheeler-Howard bill, allowed Native Americans to regain control of their people and lands within the reservation, provided that members of each reservation voted to accept these federal provisions. The Nez Perce vote resulted in their reservation opting out of the IRA. Above, chiefs of the Flathead tribe and John S. Collier watch as Harold Ickes (*seated*) signs the Wheeler-Howard bill in 1934.

addition, the IRA advocated ending the system of land allotments on reservations. It also encouraged the formation of tribal councils for local self-government that would have somewhat more authority than they had under previous federal policies. Finally, the IRA stated that in order for its provisions to become effective on any reservation, the majority of adult members of that community must vote to accept it.

Accordingly, an election was held on the Nez Perce Indian Reservation in November 1934. There was much debate and controversy on the reservation prior to the vote. Those in favor believed that the IRA would strengthen the tribe's ability to oversee its own affairs. They also hoped that the federal government would provide increased funding to support local programs. The people opposed feared that their lands would eventually be vulnerable to federal taxation. Many of the Christian Nez Perce opposed the support given by the IRA to the maintenance of traditional religious ceremonies. In this atmosphere of controversy, by a vote of 252 to 214 (with 142 members not voting), the Nez Perce chose to exclude themselves from the provisions of the Indian Reorganization Act. Although most reservation communities in the United States voted to accept the IRA, a majority of Native American groups in the Plateau and Northwest decided to reject it.

NEZ PERCE TRIBAL EXECUTIVE COMMITTEE

Despite rejecting the Indian Reorganization Act, the Nez Perce continued their efforts at developing tribal institutions and governing systems. They acted in the climate of a revised federal policy that encouraged self-government, respected tribal institutions, and supported local cultural practices. A new Nez Perce governing constitution was drafted and accepted in 1948. It established a general council consisting of all adult members of the tribe, led by the Nez Perce Tribal Executive Committee (NPTEC). The committee consisted of nine members elected by all Nez Perce adults attending the general council meeting. The committee administered a wide range of projects, including the protection and expansion of fish and water resources; social service and welfare programs in education, health, and housing; law enforcement; and legal affairs and land claims.

Although there was some opposition to the new constitution, especially because of fears of concentrating power in the NPTEC, support for it was prompted by the formation of the federal Indian Claims Commission in 1946. The commission was charged with reviewing cases brought by tribal governments against the United States for compensation for land that had been taken without treaty or had been lost from territory guaranteed by treaty. The commission was empowered to accept cases until 1952 but that date was extended until 1979. The NPTEC began to collect evidence in support of land claims and suits to protect their treaty rights.

When the Nez Perce general council was originally planned, only people who lived within the borders of the reservation as described in the Treaty of 1863 were allowed to vote for the NPTEC and to voice their opinions about tribal governance matters. But in 1961, people who lived in the wider area encompassed by the original reservation established by the Treaty of 1855 were also included in the general council. This change has created some conflicts because of the contrasting interests of people living on the current reservation and those who are living officially off the reservation. Some of the issues that divide these two groups concern plans for economic development on the reservation, the amount of power vested in the central tribal leadership of the NPTEC, the degree of necessary accommodation to federal policies on Native Americans, and funding for cultural and language heritage programs.

THREATS TO TRIBAL CONTINUITY

In the 1950s, federal policy toward reservations took a major turn with passage of several congressional bills aimed at terminating federal responsibilities to specified Native American communities. The Termination Act of 1953 named the Nez Perce, among others, to be dropped from federal services and obligations. Although the act's provisions regarding the Nez Perce were never carried out, the climate of insecurity about their long-term status undermined the community's well-being.

Then, in 1956, Congress passed the Relocation Act, whose aim was supposedly to provide job training for Native Americans in urban centers located in the Midwest and West. However, this act also undermined the stability of reservations by relocating many people away from their home communities with a consequent loss of income and talent. In the words of one Nez Perce woman included in James's collection:

> The relocation programs of the 1950s and 1960s did have tremendous impact on Indian people nationally and on the Nez Perce Tribe . . . . They created large urban populations without any sort of support system for that population . . . [And] there is a draw of skilled Indian people away from the Reservation, away from the tribal communities through education, jobs . . . Nez Perce people have now a base, a family system out there in Seattle or Portland or Los Angeles or San Francisco and other places. The Nez Perce Tribe has a lot of really talented people within the tribe, but there are a lot of talented people who are members of the tribe who are living outside.

NEZ PERCE COMMUNITIES

Beginning in the early reservation period in the late nineteenth century, various Nez Perce communities have experienced different kinds of social and political influences. The western regions of the reservation, closest to Oregon and Washington, have become socially and politically dominant. The town of Lapwai has drawn people not only from nearby western areas, but also from the eastern areas of the reservation, leading to depopulation in the east. Lapwai is located only 10 miles (16 km) from the urban centers of Lewiston-Clarkson in Idaho. In contrast, the eastern town of Kamiah has lost population. Residents of Lapwai were more receptive to influences from Anglo-American society. They were more likely to speak English rather than the Nez Perce language, and they were also more likely to marry people who were not Nez Perce.

In the late nineteenth and early twentieth centuries, Nez Perce who married outside the tribal group tended to form unions with other indigenous peoples of the Plateau and Northwest regions. Marriages with Anglo-Americans became more common as the number of whites in the community increased dramatically, beginning after 1895 when whites were permitted to live on the Nez Perce Indian

Reservation. By the middle of the twentieth century, most Nez Perce still preferred to marry other members of their own group, but marriage with whites had become a common choice as well.

Frequency of such unions varies with location. Nez Perce who live off the reservation are most likely to marry people from other groups. Among the Nez Perce who live on the reservation, those living in the west around Lapwai are more likely than people living in the eastern Kamiah region to marry members of other groups. These differences in rates of intermarriage are associated with other constellations of attitudes and behaviors. For example, Nez Perce married to other Nez Perce are more likely to retain traditional social values, especially related to family and household obligations. In contrast, Nez Perce who have married members of other groups are more likely to accept changes in their ways of living, influenced as they are by their spouses and children.

Finally, in the twentieth century, Nez Perce religious affiliations became quite complex. A significant number of Nez Perce became unhappy with the Presbyterian and Catholic churches because of these groups' support for the land allotment policies of the federal government. Some people turned to Pentecostal Protestant sects that offered dramatic and healing emotional experiences. In some ways, Pentecostal ceremonies shared features that recall the spirit quests and visions of traditional Nez Perce beliefs. Like practitioners of indigenous religions, Pentecostal believers strive to make direct contact with the spirit world through prayer, song, and movement. In addition, many Nez Perce are returning to traditional religious practices, especially seeking personal tutelary spirits through vision quests and participation in the Winter Spirit Dances and the Seven Drum Religion.

Revitalization of indigenous religions is also associated with emphases on other aspects of Nez Perce traditions. Many people have become interested in learning the Nez Perce language. Many also participate in festivals and powwows that celebrate the Nez Perce musical, visual, and dance arts. These efforts strengthen and promote people's ties to their communities.

The Nez Perce Today

The Nez Perce have created a strong and secure community after many decades of struggle and change. The people have generated a local governing body that oversees many innovative programs to help improve conditions for the people on the reservation. Economic strength is crucial to the people's well being. The maintenance of some cultural and aesthetic traditions also contributes to fostering pride in the people's past and in their future.

POPULATION CHARACTERISTICS

The Nez Perce Indian Reservation currently contains some 750,000 acres (303,500 ha) of land, but only 88,000 acres (35,600 ha) of this territory are owned by Nez Perce people. The majority of land is therefore owned by outsiders, mostly white people. Although the reservation encompasses only a small percentage of their original 13-million-acre (5,260,900-ha) homeland, it represents an increase from the 80,000-acre (32,375-ha) reservation they had in 1975 as a result of land allotments and sales. The tribe continues efforts to buy back some of the 7,500,000 acres (3,035,140 ha) of land that was originally guaranteed to them in the Treaty of 1855.

Regulations established by the Nez Perce Tribal Executive Committee (NPTEC) mandate that in order for a person to be a tribal member, he or she must have at least one-quarter Nez Perce ancestry. In 2010, there were 3,363 members of the Nez Perce Tribe. This number varies somewhat with statistics reported by the U.S. Bureau of the Census in the year 2000. According to census data, there are currently 4,082 Nez Perce residents of the reservation. The Census Bureau also reports that Nez Perce Indians account for only 11.7 percent of the reservation population, while white people (numbering 15,186) make up 84.6 percent, a vast majority. People of other races make up the remainder.

Age distribution statistics reveal that 8.1 percent of the Nez Perce living on the reservation are children under the age of 5 years. At the other end of the lifespan, only 0.5 percent are 85 years of age or older. These figures contrast significantly with comparable figures for the U.S. population as a whole, but they are similar to figures for reservations in the country. In the United States as a whole, 6.8 percent of all residents are under the age of 5 years, while 1.5 percent are age 85 or older. In other words, the Nez Perce population is a relatively youthful one compared to the rest of the United States. This conclusion is borne out by comparing data for median age. Among the Nez Perce, the median age is 30.1 years, while the general U.S. figure is 35.3 years.

A comparison of Nez Perce family and household organization reveals some interesting contrasts between the Nez Perce and U.S. totals. Nez Perce families have more children and younger children than the general U.S. population. There are also fewer Nez Perce households with elderly people than in the United States as a whole. Another interesting contrast is that there are fewer Nez

Perce individuals living alone. Looked at another way, Nez Perce households are larger than in American society generally. The Nez Perce average household size is 3.0, compared to a total U.S. figure of 2.59.

Data for married couples and single-parent households also reveal contrasts. A significantly larger percentage of American families consist of married couples (51.7 percent) than among the Nez Perce (41.5 percent). Among the Nez Perce, a higher percentage of households are headed by women with no husband present (19.9 percent) than elsewhere in the United States (12.2 percent). Finally, of all the Nez Perce households in which grandparents are living in the same dwelling as one or more of their own grandchildren under the age of 18, 56.8 percent of these grandparents are responsible for their grandchildren's care.

EMPLOYMENT AND INCOME DATA

Economic and employment data collected by the Bureau of the Census for the year 2000 indicate higher rates of unemployment for the Nez Perce than in the United States as a whole, and correspondingly lower levels of income. In that year, of the 2,998 Nez Perce living on the reservation who were 16 years and older, 63.4 percent were eligible to work: 55.9 percent were employed while 7.5 percent were unemployed. The remaining 36.6 percent were not in the labor force either because they did not want to work or because they were discouraged workers no longer looking for jobs.

The most striking contrast between the Nez Perce and the American population as a whole is the percentage of unemployed people. Although nearly the same percentage of Nez Perce and all Americans were in the labor force (63.4 percent for the Nez Perce and 63.9 percent for all Americans), the Nez Perce unemployment rate was double that of the United States (7.5 percent for the Nez Perce and 3.7 percent for the United States as a whole).

The following list presents the percentages of Nez Perce employed in various occupations:

Management, professional, and related occupations	28.4 percent
Service	24.1 percent
Sales and office	24.7 percent
Farming, fishing, and forestry	1.6 percent
Construction, extraction, and maintenance	7.0 percent
Production, transportation, and moving	14.3 percent

Finally, of all Nez Perce workers, 59.2 percent worked for private businesses or organizations, while 36.7 percent worked for the federal or tribal governments. Indeed, tribal governmental agencies and enterprises are a major reservation employer. An additional 4.1 percent were self-employed workers.

Statistics reporting income indicate that Nez Perce workers and families have relatively low earnings as compared to the general U.S. population. In the year 2000, 17.4 percent of Nez Perce households had annual incomes of less than $10,000, while only 9.5 percent of all Americans had similarly low incomes. At the other end of the income spectrum, only 2.2 percent of Nez Perce households had incomes of between $100,000 and $150,000 per year, compared to 7.7 percent for the United States. No Nez Perce tribal member had an income above $200,000, while 2.4 percent of all Americans had such high incomes. Finally, the Nez Perce median family income for that year stood at $33,846, in contrast to the U.S. median family income, which was $50,046. For the Nez Perce, per capita income was $12,817, while the U.S. per capita income stood at $21,587. Consistent with the general American pattern, Nez Perce male workers earned more than female workers: The median income for men working full-time year round was $28,516, while for women the comparable figure was $22,274.

Given the generally low incomes of Nez Perce families, the poverty rate for the year 2000 was relatively high. Some 17.5 percent of Nez Perce families were living below the poverty level. Families with children suffered even more: Families with children under the age of 18 had a poverty rate of 22.5 percent and families

Living on a reservation presents a unique set of challenges and obstacles to Native Americans. The population on the Nez Perce reservation (*above*) has double the unemployment rate of the rest of the United States, as well as a lower rate of income.

with children younger than 5 years of age had a poverty rate of 32.3 percent.

Again consistent with general American trends, families headed by women with no husband present had still higher poverty rates: 34.4 percent of all such families lived below the poverty level. Nearly half (44.9 percent) of families headed by women with children under the age of 18 lived below the poverty level, while more than two-thirds (66.7 percent) of such families with children younger than 5 years of age were poor. Many individuals living alone also experienced high rates of poverty. Nearly one-quarter (23.3 percent) of such people lived below the poverty level. The poverty rate for Nez Perce families is nearly double that of families in the general U.S. population. Poverty rates for female-headed households are also much higher than for similar households in the United States as a whole.

POPULATION SOCIAL CHARACTERISTICS

In addition to reporting household organization and economic data, the Bureau of the Census collects information about certain social characteristics of a population. For example, statistics on education reveal that the Nez Perce are somewhat better educated than the U.S. population in general at the high school and community college level, but are less well-educated at the level of four-year college and graduate degrees. Slightly less than one-fifth (18.7 percent) of all Nez Perce members 25 years or older have not completed high school, compared to a U.S. norm of 19.6 percent. About 30 percent of the Nez Perce are high school graduates and another 30 percent have attended college but have not received a degree. (The comparable U.S. figures are 28.6 percent high school graduates and 21.1 percent attending college without receiving a degree.) Finally, 7.2 percent of the Nez Perce have their associate's degree (6.3 percent for the U.S. total), 8.2 percent have a bachelor's degree from a four-year college (15.5 percent for the U.S. total), and 5.1 percent have graduate school or professional degrees (8.9 percent for the U.S. total).

Data on marriage reveal that 43.6 percent of the Nez Perce population 15 years and older were married in the year 2000. About one-third (33.2 percent) were never married, while about one-fifth (19.2 percent) were separated or divorced and 3.9 percent were widowed. Nearly all of the Nez Perce who were widowed were women (3.4 percent).

TRIBAL GOVERNANCE AND AGENCIES

The Nez Perce Tribal Executive Committee, with a current membership of four women and five men, has spearheaded the expansion of economic, social, and legal services to its communities. It has established a number of agencies to deal with specific issues.

Some of these agencies have the goal of expanding employment and economic development. For example, the Tribal Employment Rights Commission, according to its mission statement, ". . . advocates for the development of employment and training opportunities for a skilled Nez Perce workforce and creates positive economic impacts on the Reservation." The commission draws up regulations for the conduct of business and establishes procedures for certifying Native American businesses, helping in the application process.

The Land Enterprise Commission has two goals: to generate income for the Nez Perce Tribe by leasing land on the reservation and to purchase additional acreage next to the reservation in order to accomplish territorial expansion. Funds received by the Nez Perce Tribe are administered through the Budget and Finance Subcommittee. This group solicits and approves contracts for various kinds of projects benefiting the tribe. The Nez Perce Tribal Gaming Commission is charged with regulating gaming operations at two casinos run by the tribe: the Clearwater River Casino and the It'se Ye Ye Bingo and Casino. These casinos must comply with regulations both of the federal National Indian Gaming Regulatory Act of 1988 and the Nez Perce Tribal Gaming Ordinance.

In order to protect Nez Perce lands and resources, the Natural Resources Subcommittee declares its goal to "expand and protect our precious natural resources, which are fundamental to who we are as a people." In so doing, the subcommittee also protects rights of access to natural resources both on and off the reservation as guaranteed by the treaties of 1855, 1863, and 1868. They direct programs dealing with fisheries, forestry, water resources, wildlife, tourism, and environmental restoration and waste management. All of these various programs and offices are charged with protecting and expanding the natural resources of the Nez Perce Indian Reservation as well as developing projects for their sustainable use.

The Natural Resources Subcommittee directs the Cultural Resource Program that aims to protect and enhance Nez Perce control over cultural and historical resources. These include efforts by the tribe to regain ownership of important cultural artifacts that were taken illegally or sold to private collectors or museums in the past. Since Congress passed the Native American Grave and Repatriation Act in 1990, Native American tribes have been empowered to seek restoration or "repatriation" of skeletal remains and religious and cultural objects taken from them in the nineteenth and twentieth centuries.

The act outlines a complex series of procedures that tribes must comply with and criteria that tribes must satisfy in order to repatriate their cultural objects. The procedures can take many years to complete. In 2009, the federal government issued its "Notice of Intent" to repatriate several objects, including human remains and funerary artifacts, to the Nez Perce that were held by the U.S. Department of Defense and Army Corps of Engineers, and housed in museums at the University of Washington and the University of California at Berkeley.

Health and education are fundamental concerns of the Nez Perce community. The Human Resources Subcommittee implements programs to improve enrollment in schools, acquires additional funds for education, and awards scholarships to Nez Perce students who want to attend college and graduate degree programs. The subcommittee also oversees the Nimiipuu Health Board that administers programs dealing with health and wellness. The tribe has opened a new health facility, hired additional doctors, and expanded services to the community.

Finally, the Nez Perce government has established a tribal court that has jurisdiction (legal power) on the reservation, on areas that consist of the "usual and accustomed fishing locations of the Nez Perce Tribe," and on "open and unclaimed lands." The tribal court has a complex set of jurisdictions. It has criminal jurisdiction over all crimes committed by any Native American within the Nez Perce Indian Reservation; over actions that violate Nez Perce fish and game laws at any of the "usual and accustomed fishing places" used by the Nez Perce; and over civil actions to which "an Indian or Indian owned property is a party." In addition, the tribal court has civil jurisdiction over any person living on or present on the reservation; any person conducting business within the reservation either in person or through mail or telephone; and any person owning or using property within the reservation.

Actions by the tribal court, like all other Native American courts in the United States, operate under some restrictions given the limited sovereignty that tribes enjoy. For the Nez Perce, the court acts in accordance with its own tribal laws and codes of behavior, "except to the extent that Federal law governs." The most important restrictions come from congressional laws, especially the Major Crimes Act, originally passed in 1885 and amended in 1976. The acts together mandate that cases on reservations involving the crimes of murder, kidnapping, manslaughter, rape, incest, several types of assault, arson, burglary, robbery, and larceny are to be prosecuted in federal courts. Tribal courts may have jurisdiction over other crimes as they see fit.

The Nez Perce tribal court is headed by a chief justice and has several associate judges, all appointed by the Nez Perce Tribal Executive Committee. The court also has a Native American child welfare worker responsible for ensuring the care or custody of children under its protection. Caseworkers and social workers are employed to protect the rights of individuals and families coming under the jurisdiction of the court.

In order to both generate income and expand people's knowledge of Nez Perce history, the tribe opened the Nez Perce National Historical Park with sites both on the reservation and outside its current boundaries. There are 38 sites that commemorate the location of battlefields, trading posts, missions, and forts. The trails and campsites used by Chief Joseph and his followers in their attempt to escape from U.S. Army control are also marked. Finally, significant locations in Nez Perce culture are highlighted, including the site of ancient petroglyphs and the places described in sacred narratives such as the "Heart of the Monster," where Coyote killed the Monster and released the Nez Perce people into this world.

Located on the Nez Perce National Historical Park, ancient petroglyphs drawn on cave walls depict the creation of the Nez Perce. Hundreds of unique images can be found throughout the park's 38 sites, including a few that are 4,500 years old.

LAND AND RESOURCE CLAIMS CASES

The Nez Perce Tribe is an active participant in several regional coalitions concerned with protecting indigenous people's fishing and resource rights as guaranteed in numerous treaties signed in the nineteenth century. In the 1950s, they participated, along with representatives of the Yakama, Umatilla, and Warm Springs nations, in negotiations with the U.S. Army Corps of Engineers in a dispute over compensation for the loss of fishing sites in the area known as Celilo Falls in Oregon. These sites were principal fishing locations for the Nez Perce and other regional indigenous peoples for thousands of years, but were under threat of flooding from the construction of the Dalles Dam, completed in 1957. Finally, after years of negotiations, the tribes were awarded a total of about $27 million. The Nez Perce received $2,800,000 from this settlement, a direct compensation for loss of fishing sites. The Nez Perce continue to insist on their rights to fish in their "usual and accustomed places" as guaranteed by treaty with the U.S. government.

Then, in 1977, Nez Perce representatives took part in founding the Columbia River Inter-Tribal Fish Commission, a network of indigenous peoples in the Northwest whose goal is the protection and rehabilitation of the rivers and streams that are critical to the preservation of salmon and steelhead trout runs. These runs are, in turn, critical to the livelihood, sense of identity, and cultural integrity of Nez Perce people.

After nearly 10 years of negotiations, the Nez Perce Tribe came to an agreement with the U.S. Department of the Interior and the State of Idaho in 2007 over claims to use of the Snake River waters. The Nez Perce claim stems from the treaties of 1855 and 1863 that guaranteed the people enough water for uses on the reservation. The Treaty of 1855 also guaranteed fishing rights in "all usual and accustomed places" not only on the reservation but also on the lands that the Nez Perce ceded to the U.S. government in that treaty. Finally, the Treaty of 1863 grants the Nez Perce the right to use any springs or fountains that are located in the area that

The Importance of Salmon

Salmon play an integral part of tribal religion, culture, and physical sustenance. Below is a short list of the many ways that the tribes consider the salmon to be sacred, written by the Columbia River Inter-Tribal Fish Commission.

- Salmon are part of our spiritual and cultural identity.
- Over a dozen longhouses and churches on the reservations and in ceded areas rely on salmon for their religious services.
- The annual salmon return and its celebration by our peoples assures the renewal and continuation of human and all other life.
- Historically, we were wealthy peoples because of a flourishing trade economy based on salmon.
- For many tribal members, fishing is still the preferred livelihood.
- Salmon and the rivers they use are part of our sense of place. The Creator put us here where the salmon return. We are obliged to remain and to protect this place.
- Salmon are an indicator species: As water becomes degraded and fish populations decline, so too will the elk, deer, roots, berries, and medicines that sustain us.
- As a primary food source for thousands of years, salmon continue to be an essential aspect of our nutritional health.
- Because our tribal populations are growing (returning to pre-1855 levels), the needs for salmon are more important than ever.
- The annual return of the salmon allows the transfer of traditional values from generation to generation.
- Without salmon returning to our rivers and streams, we would cease to be Indian people.

The route Chief Joseph and his followers took while fleeing the U.S. army in 1877 was declared a National Historic Trail in 1986. The trail begins in Oregon and travels through parts of Idaho, Montana, and Wyoming. Above, a commemorative parade on the Nez Perce Trail heads toward Bear Paw Battlefield, Montana, for a memorial ceremony.

was first guaranteed as their reservation in the 1855 Treaty before being ceded to the government in the Treaty of 1863.

The water rights agreement, called the Snake River Basin Adjudication, grants the Nez Perce Tribe the right to consume water from the Clearwater River and some tributary sources. They were also granted claims to springs and fountains on federal lands within the area ceded in the Treaty of 1863, but were denied their claims to springs on lands within that area if controlled by the

State of Idaho or private owners. In addition, certain lands under the control of the federal Bureau of Land Management, valued at $7 million, were given to the Nez Perce Tribe. The tribe was established as co-manager, along with federal agencies, of national fish hatcheries. Finally, the tribe received $73 million for the acquisition and restoration of lands for fish habitats, fish production, agricultural development, water resource development, sewer and water system projects, and cultural preservation projects.

Land and resource issues of today are linked historically to the exploratory expedition led by Meriwether Lewis and William Clark more than 200 years ago. That expedition opened the way for traders, settlers, missionaries, and government officials. The policies and actions of these outsiders resulted in the loss of millions of acres of land once held by the Nez Perce and led to fundamental cultural changes. Some contemporary Nez Perce leaders participated in 2004 in national events marking the two-hundredth anniversary of the Lewis and Clark expeditions. The numerous trails that the expedition followed across Nez Perce territory are part of the Nez Perce National Historical Trail Park, a major tourist attraction in the region. Allen Pinkham, a Nez Perce member of the National Lewis and Clark Bicentennial Council, raised concerns about the programs: "The general population wants to see heroes, and to them Lewis and Clark are heroes. To us, they mean something completely different." Clara HighEagle, a member of the Nez Perce Tribal Executive Committee, noted that the bicentennial should be "commemorated, not celebrated."

With tribal programs and other initiatives, the Nez Perce of the twenty-first century dedicate themselves to strengthening their communities and enlarging their land base through purchases of acreage once included in the original reservation in the treaties of 1855 and 1863. They acknowledge the cultural achievements and uniqueness of their indigenous ancestors. They know the importance of understanding their history so that they can protect their rights to the resources of their lands, and they develop projects that ensure their security and prosperity for generations to come.

Chronology

2500 b.c.	Direct ancestors of the modern Nez Perce settle in their homelands in territory that is now part of central and western Idaho, eastern Oregon, and eastern Washington.
c. 1720	Nez Perce begin acquiring horses through trade with other indigenous peoples, including the Shoshone and Flathead, who themselves had obtained the animals from Spanish traders and settlers in what later became known as the American Southwest.
1774	First documented smallpox epidemic in Nez Perce communities. The epidemic is estimated to have led to the deaths of about 40 percent of the Nez Perce population.
1801–1802	A second deadly wave of smallpox costs additional Nez Perce lives. More lives were lost in subsequent bouts of the disease in 1853 and 1862.
1805–1806	An American exploratory expedition led by Meriwether Lewis and William Clark arrives in Nez Perce territory; they spend several months with the Nez Perce.
1812	North West Company, a British fur trading company, opens a trading post in Nez Perce territory.
1829	The Rocky Mountain Fur Company, an American trading company, opens a trading post in Nez Perce territory.
1836	Presbyterian mission is established by Henry Spalding at Lapwai Creek in Nez Perce territory.
1840s	Day schools and boarding schools open in Nez Perce communities to begin the process of transforming Nez Perce culture to conform with American norms and ideals.

1855   Walla Walla Treaty is signed between the Nez Perce, other indigenous peoples of the Plateau, and the U.S. government.

1862   Gold is discovered in and near Nez Perce territories, leading to the influx of more than 10,000 American settlers. As a result, the government put pressure on the Nez Perce to give up more of their land.

1863   A number of Nez Perce leaders agree to a second treaty with the U.S. government, which takes away more than 7 million acres (2,832,800 ha) from the original reservation. This leaves the Nez Perce with only 757,000 acres (306,350 ha).

1868   A third treaty between the Nez Perce and the U.S. government clarifies some of the provisions of the Treaty of 1863.

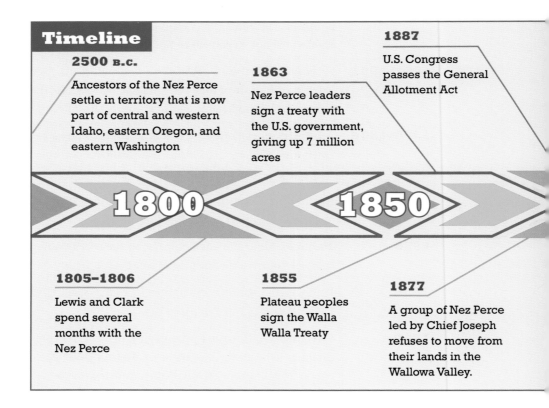

Timeline

2500 B.C.
Ancestors of the Nez Perce settle in territory that is now part of central and western Idaho, eastern Oregon, and eastern Washington

1863
Nez Perce leaders sign a treaty with the U.S. government, giving up 7 million acres

1887
U.S. Congress passes the General Allotment Act

1800   **1850**

1805–1806
Lewis and Clark spend several months with the Nez Perce

1855
Plateau peoples sign the Walla Walla Treaty

1877
A group of Nez Perce led by Chief Joseph refuses to move from their lands in the Wallowa Valley.

1877   A group of Nez Perce led by Chief Joseph refuses to move from their lands in the Wallowa Valley. A three-month series of battles and retreats eventually led to the surrender of Chief Joseph just 40 miles (65 km) south of the Canadian border where his group was seeking refuge.

1886   After spending about seven years on the Ponca Reservation in Oklahoma, survivors of Chief Joseph's band are relocated to the Colville Reservation in Washington, sharing that land with other indigenous peoples of the Northwest.

1887   U.S. Congress passes the Dawes Severalty Act.

1890   Provisions of the General Allotment Act go into effect on the Nez Perce Reservation.

1893   Under pressure by the U.S. government, Nez Perce leaders agree to sell additional acres of "surplus" lands.

1895

President Grover Cleveland opens all unclaimed lands on the Nez Perce Indian Reservation to settlement by American homesteaders, ranchers, and farmers

1957

The Nez Perce and the Yakama, Umatilla, and Warm Springs nations sue the federal government for flooding many of their fishing sites

1900   **2000**

1927

The Nez Perce pass their first governing constitution

1977

Nez Perce representatives take part in founding the Columbia River Inter-Tribal Fish Commission

2007

The Nez Perce agree to a settlement of their claims to use of waters from the Snake and Clearwater rivers, guaranteeing rights to water from rivers that flow through the reservation

1895 U.S. president Grover Cleveland issues a decree that opens all unclaimed and unallotted lands on the Nez Perce Indian Reservation to settlement by American homesteaders, ranchers, and farmers.

1922 The Nez Perce form the Nez Perce Indian Home and Farm Association.

1927 The Nez Perce draft and pass their first governing constitution.

1934 The Nez Perce population votes 252 to 214 to reject the provisions of the Indian Reorganization Act.

1948 The Nez Perce draft and accept a second governing constitution.

1957 The Dalles Dam in Oregon is completed; the Nez Perce, along with representatives of other Native American groups, sue the federal government for compensation.

1977 Nez Perce representatives take part in founding the Columbia River Inter-Tribal Fish Commission.

2007 After nearly 10 years of negotiations, the Nez Perce Tribe agrees to a settlement of its claims to use of waters from the Snake and Clearwater rivers.

Glossary

Archaeologist   A researcher who gathers information about a people's lifestyle from the material objects that they leave behind, such as their housing, tools, clothing, and artwork

Bilateral kinship   A system of family relationships in which people consider themselves related through both their mother's family and their father's family

Egalitarian principles   Social and economic principles that consider people to be equal in their rights and responsibilities

Extended family   Family unit made up of three or more generations; for example, grandparents, parents, and their children

Foraging   An economic system based on gathering wild plants and hunting animals

Indigenous people   The first inhabitants of a territory who were living in a region prior to the arrival of foreign settlers

Kindred   An informal grouping of people who consider themselves relatives

Menstrual lodge   A structure for girls and women to use during their menstrual periods

Missionary   A member of a religious group who attempts to persuade other people to join that religion

Nuclear family   Family unit made up of a married couple and their children

Population density   The number of people living in a specific area of land

Reservation   A territory set aside for members of a Native American group, guaranteed by treaty between the United States and the group in question

Rites of passage   Ceremonies that celebrate significant changes in the life cycle, such as birth, puberty, marriage, and death

Subsistence activities   The methods by which people obtain their food

Sweat lodge   A structure designed to produce steam by heating rocks and then pouring water over them; people used sweat lodges for rituals to purify their bodies

Treaty   An official, legal agreement between two or more nations that sets out specific issues about their relationship

Tutelary spirits   Spirit helpers that people obtain through prayer and fasting in order to receive personal protection and guidance

Visionary quests   Rituals that people perform in order to receive tutelary spirit assistance

Bibliography

Ames, Kenneth, Don Dumond, Jerry Galm, and Rick Minor. "Prehistory of the Southern Plateau." *Plateau.* Handbook of North American Indians. Vol. 12. Washington, D.C.: Smithsonian Institution, 1998.

Aoki, Haruo. "Nez Perce Texts." *Nez Perce Dictionary.* University of California Publications in Linguistics. Vol. 90. Berkeley: University of California Press, 1994.

Beal, Merrill D. *"I Will Fight No More Forever": Chief Joseph and the Nez Perce War.* Seattle: University of Washington Press, 1963.

Beckham, Stephen. "History Since 1846." Plateau. Handbook of North American Indians. Vol. 12. Washington, D.C.: Smithsonian Institution, 1998.

Boyd, Robert. "Smallpox in the Pacific Northwest: The First Epidemics." *BC Studies, The British Columbian Quarterly* 101 (Spring 1994): 5–40.

Chatters, James and David Pokotylo. "Prehistory: Introduction." *Plateau.* Handbook of North American Indians. Vol. 12. Washington, D.C.: Smithsonian Institution, 1998.

Davis, Mary, ed. *Native America in the Twentieth Century.* New York: Garland Publishing, 1994.

Haines, Francis. "How the Indian Got the Horse." *American Heritage,* February 1964. Available online. URL: http://www.americanheritage. com/articles/magazine/ah/1964/2/1964_2_16.shtml.

Hunn, Eugene, Nancy Turner, and David French. "Ethnobiology and Subsistence." *Plateau.* Handbook of North American Indians. Vol. 12. Washington, D.C.: Smithsonian Institution, 1998.

James, Caroline. *Nez Perce Women in Transition, 1877–1990.* Moscow: University of Idaho Press, 1996.

James, Darcy. "The Continuing Impact of Manifest Destiny in a Small Town." *Wacazo Sa Review* 14, no. 1 (Spring 1999): 147–163.

Josephy, Alvin. *The Nez Perce Indians and the Opening of the Northwest.* New Haven: Yale University Press, 1965.

Lahren, Sylvester. "Reservations and Service." *Plateau.* Handbook of North American Indians. Vol. 12. Washington, D.C.: Smithsonian Institution, 1998.

Lavender, David. *Let Me Be Free: The Nez Perce Tragedy.* New York: Harper-Collins, 1992.

Moulton, Gary, ed. *The Journals of the Lewis and Clark Expedition, July 28–November 1, 1805.* Lincoln: University of Nebraska Press, 1988.

Moulton, Gary, ed. *The Journals of the Lewis and Clark Expedition, November 2, 1805–March 22, 1806.* Lincoln: University of Nebraska Press, 1990.

Sappington, Robert. "The Lewis and Clark Expedition Among the Nez Perce Indians: The First Ethnographic Study in the Columbia Plateau." *Northwest Anthropological Research Notes* 23, no. 1 (1989): 1–33.

Slickpoo, Allen and Deward Walker. *Noon Nee-me-poo (We, The Nez Perces): Culture and History of the Nez Perces.* Vol. 1. Lapwai: Nez Perce Tribe of Idaho, 1973.

Slickpoo, Allen, Leroy Seth, and Deward Walker. *Nu Mee Poom Tit Wah Tit. (Nez Perce Legends).* 3rd ed. Lapwai: Nez Perce Tribe of Idaho, 1975.

Stern, Theodore. "Columbia River Trade Network." *Handbook of North American Indians, Volume 12: Plateau,* Washington, D.C.: Smithsonian Institution, 1998.

Walker, Deward. *American Indians of Idaho.* Anthropology Monographs of the University of Idaho, Vol. 1 (2). Moscow: Idaho Research Foundation, 1973.

Walker, Deward. *Conflict and Schism in Nez Perce Acculturation: A Study of Religion and Politics.* Portland: Washington State University Press, 1968.

Walker, Deward. *Myths of Idaho Indians.* Moscow: University of Idaho Press, 1982.

Walker, Deward. "Nez Perce." *Handbook of North American Indians, Volume 12: Plateau.* Washington: Smithsonian Institution, 1998.

Walker, Deward and William C. Sturtevant, eds. *Plateau.* Handbook of North American Indians. Vol. 12. Washington, D.C.: Smithsonian Institution, 1998.

Walker, Deward and Helen Schuster. "Religious Movements." *Plateau.* Handbook of North American Indians. Vol. 12. Washington, D.C.: Smithsonian Institution, 1998.

Walker, Deward and Richard Sprague. "History Until 1846." *Plateau.* Handbook of North American Indians. Vol. 12. Washington, D.C.: Smithsonian Institution, 1998.

Further Resources

McCoy, Robert. *Chief Joseph, Yellow Wolf, and the Creation of Nez Perce History in the Pacific Northwest.* London: Taylor and Francis, 2004.

Nerburn, Kent. *Chief Joseph and the Flight of the Nez Perce.* New York: HarperCollins Publishers, 2006.

Schofield, Brian. *Selling Your Father's Bones: America's 140-Year War Against the Nez Perce Tribe.* New York: Simon and Schuster, 2009.

West, Elliott. *The Last Indian War: The Nez Perce Story.* New York: Oxford University Press, 2009.

Wilfong, Cheryl. *Following the Nez Perce Trail: A Guide to the Nee-mee-Poo National Historic Trail with Eyewitness Accounts.* Corvallis: Oregon State University Press, 2006.

Web sites

Columbia River Inter-Tribal Fish Commission
www.critfc.org
This is the official Web site of the Columbia River Inter-Tribal Fish Commission, with reports about their goals, programs, and resources.

Lewis and Clark Trail
http://lewisandclarktrail.com
Following in the footsteps of Meriwether Lewis and William Clark, starting from Washington, D.C., and reaching all the way to Washington State, this site provides information about the people and places the explorers encountered. There is a photo gallery, journal entries, a virtual tour, and lesson plans for teachers and students.

National Native American Grave Repatriation Act
www.nps.gov/history/nagpra
This Web site has information about cases involving tribal claims for the return of sacred objects and cultural artifacts as guaranteed by the Native American Grave Repatriation Act.

Native American Rights Fund

www.narf.org/cases/nezperce.html

This Web site has information about lawsuits undertaken by the Native American Rights Fund for protection of tribal treaty rights.

The Nez Perce Tribe

www.nezperce.org

This is the official Web site of the Nez Perce tribe, with information about location, history, programs, and services.

Sequoyah Research Center, American Native Press Archives

www.anpa.ualr.edu

This is a Web site of a number of Native American media sources.

Picture Credits

Index

About the Contributors

Author **NANCY BONVILLAIN** received her Ph.D. in anthropology and linguistics from Columbia University. Her major fields of research and writing include Native American cultures and histories and Iroquoian linguistics. She has prepared teaching materials for the Mohawk language, in addition to writing four textbooks: *Cultural Anthropology; Language, Culture, and Communication; Native Nations;* and *Women and Men: cultural constructs of gender.* Dr. Bonvillain has written several books on Native American societies and leaders for Chelsea House.

Series editor **PAUL C. ROSIER** received his Ph.D. in American History from the University of Rochester in 1998. Dr. Rosier currently serves as Associate Professor of History at Villanova University (Villanova, Pennsylvania), where he teaches Native American History, American Environmental History, Global Environmental Justice Movements, History of American Capitalism, and World History.

In 2001 the University of Nebraska Press published his first book, *Rebirth of the Blackfeet Nation, 1912–1954;* in 2003, Greenwood Press published *Native American Issues* as part of its Contemporary Ethnic American Issues series. In 2006 he co-edited an international volume called *Echoes from the Poisoned Well: Global Memories of Environmental Injustice.* Dr. Rosier has also published articles in the *American Indian Culture and Research Journal,* the *Journal of American Ethnic History,* and *The Journal of American History.* His *Journal of American History* article, entitled "'They Are Ancestral Homelands: Race, Place, and Politics in Cold War Native America, 1945–1961," was selected for inclusion in *The Ten Best History Essays of 2006–2007,* published by Palgrave MacMillan in 2008; and it won the Western History Association's 2007 Arrell Gibson Award for Best Essay on the history of Native Americans. In 2009 Harvard University Press published his latest book, *Serving Their Country: American Indian Politics and Patriotism in the Twentieth Century.*